THE FLAMES OF WRATH

For Marion & Buster
Best regards
Ron Wilson
October 2010.

Ronald Wilson

authorHOUSE®

AuthorHouse™ UK Ltd.
500 Avebury Boulevard
Central Milton Keynes, MK9 2BE
www.authorhouse.co.uk
Phone: 08001974150

First published by AuthorHouse   10/1/2010

ISBN: 978-1-4490-5765-7 (sc)

Front Cover photo by : Carmen Mardiros

This book is printed on acid-free paper.

That day, the Day of Wrath, will turn the world to ashes.
Thomas o Celano.

Vengance is Mine, and retribution. In due time their foot will slip.
For the day of their calamity is near. And the impending things are
hastening upon them.
Deuteronomy 32;35.

I. THE LIFT.

Like a drift of mist they'd come in over the lip of the glen. No one saw them, as they'd intended, for that was their way, not to be seen and not to be heard. Everyone, of the sixteen of them, had been hand picked by MacIain. All were veteran cattle lifters, with the exception of young Achtriachtan, who had only been at it for two seasons, but he had learned quickly, for it was in his genes.

There were those who thought Mac Iain was more comfortable in the night, a creature of the dark, for he could find his way when no other could.

Darkness was falling now, the twilight before night. Higher, up the hill, grouse churred. The men halted at MacIain's signal, in order to listen. There was no sound other than the Lyon dashing through its gorges to the sea. Far off a dog barked.

A single star lit, unblinking.

Sharp, insistently, a peewit called. All knew it for MacIain's signal. With care they went on until the land flattened out into a water meadow, where cattle would graze.

An owl hooted twice, MacIain again. They halted, knowing he would go on alone to ascertain if any beasts were stanced there. Quarter of an hour later the owl called again, soft and low, once, twice, a pause and then again. Beasts were there for the taking. Silently they went on, their deer hide brogans making no sound. No man spoke. Each knew that on either hand, at fifteen to twenty paces, there would be another of the Clan. On they went, all at the same measured pace. Next would come the cough of a raven, short, sharp, and sudden.

Came the cough and they halted. MacIain would be near. The cough again and they homed in on it, working left or right, till all were met. With practised care they all stood still. Quiet as a mouse MacIain walked around them. Each extended his right arm, which the Chief touched in turn. At the count he knew that none were missing.

Three high, thin whistles and the four collies were off. Best of all dogs, with their innate herding skills and intelligence. They the silent ones; they would not yelp. Within five minutes they had cut out twenty-seven cattle and brought them back. Swiftly; MacIain concluded that this was too many. At once nine were shed. This would delay any pursuit, for the people who came on them would think the others had strayed and would search about for them; besides, for sixteen men, twenty seven would have been cumbersome; harder to drive off at speed.

They took them, north, into the wastes of Rannoch, a land that no man wanted, but, where, in its vastness, lurked outlaws; men who had been banished by their Clans and who had gone there to live, so that they would not be hunted down. The Broken Men they called them, hard and without pity, as hard as the land they now called home, Magadan na Noine, the Plain of the Moss

As was the practise, every mile or so, three men would take up the rear guard, to lie low, to check on and delay any pursuit, should it occur, whilst the others went on with the lifted cattle. A quarter of an hour later a new rear guard would be in place and in a leapfrog movement the previous guard would go on to join the main drive.

Morning was coming. In the east, slowly, the sky lightened, and, as the sun rose, the air was charged with light, which lay on the land, soft as thistle down. Around was mile upon mile of endless nothing, loch and lochan, rock and bog, heather and deer cut peat hag and an emptiness of living things, land without limit. There was no sound, no shred of wind not a single whisper, no fall of water, only the totality of a vast silence.

It was time for rest and a bite to eat. When they had done so MacIain sent them on again, northwest for Glencoe. He himself, Tearlach Og and young Achtriachtan made up the rear guard.

Curlews began to call, their music ululating over the moor. Time went on and they had to go, so the three set off to link up with the main group. Before them stood a small clump of birches, shameless, a trifle wanton, so beautiful, with an exquisite translucency of leaf, which had all the transparency of a maiden's diaphanous robe. As they passed a gun banged, its muzzle flash a bloom of yellow. Four men ran at them, swords drawn.

"Run you, Achtriachtan, run", MacIain called out.

Tearlach Og was down, gun shot. Full of deadly purpose, at the run, the four came on, shouts of threat and anger pouring from them.

As the first to arrive lifted his blade to strike, MacIain's back handed sword stroke took him full on the neck, he dropped at once, blood spurting from him. There was no time for reasoned thought At his full height, with his great reach, the Chief knew he had the best of them, but, with three to contend with and nowhere to put his back for protection, he would be busy. At once he started to circle, keeping them moving in a ring. They danced and slashed. He thrust and parried, the swords ringing and clanging as they clashed.

One man broke off and began to load his musket, pouring powder from a flask. That would be fatal, MacIain knew.

Suddenly, there was a great shout of "Eilean Fraoch", and young Achtriachtan burst from the trees, and, swift as lightning, dirked the gunman.

It was over with that, the two enemies, who were capable, breaking off and running.

"Let them go", said MacIain. "They are a long way from home and seem to have no other company. Glenorchy's Laird's men by the hue of their tartan".

They looked to Tearlach , who was lying on his back, his eyes closed, the front of his shirt soaked with blood. Quickly, the Chief cut the shirt open. There was a gaping wound on the lower right hand side of his ribcage, from which blood was welling.

"Pull a handful of yon spagnum moss, not the green, but the withered white"

At once the young lad did so.

MacIain placed it over the wound and secured it with a strip of cloth. With care he turned Tearlach over. There was no exit wound.

"The ball is still in him".

Just then a froth of tiny red bubbles appeared on the injured man's lips. His face was chalk white.

"He is lung shot", thought the Chief.

"Laddie, there is only one thing for it. If the shot was not heard by our men, you must go for Glencoe; for if he lives it will only be by the bullet being cut out. Try to catch our men, but I have my doubts of that, for they'll still be running the beasts, and they could be the best part of six miles off by now. Make for Maurice Begg's house, below the Meeting of the Three waters, and have them send for Beaton the Surgeon. If Tearlach lives it will be best that he see to him"

At that, young Achtriachtan was off at the lope, into the gathering mist.   MacIain examined the dead assailant; there was no doubting he wore Glenorchy's tartan.

With care the Chief hid his sword, dirk, and sporran of meal, marking the spot in his mind's eye, with a view to their subsequent recovery. His skian dubh and his flask were all he retained; everything else he shed; Tearlach Og would be weight enough.

The Pulse was weak and erratic. With care MacIain picked the wounded man up and put him on his back, setting off, with his burden, north-west for Glencoe.

Before him the moor went on forever, stretching into eternity; a great toil of weariness. On he went, hour after hour, stopping now and then to check Tearlach's condition, and for rest. As he went the bog sucked at his feet, the dark mud coating his brogans and legs. Each step became a trial, His shoulder muscles, his leg muscles, the muscles in his back began to cry out. His chest was aflame. All he felt was pain.

Tearlach had ceased to bleed, but the furnace of his lung, where the ball had torn through, was ablaze with hot searing agony. He was slowly going, MacIain concluded. His breathing had become more forced. His eyes were tight shut, little beads of sweat having formed on his cheeks.

Horizon and sky made a bold sweep, bare and boundless the distance, the rising wind in his face, the mist lifting with it and the utter desolation; the bareness and the totality of it, an all-encompassing desert, strove to lay its bleakness on his soul. Mist lay low on the land, thick and white, only the high tops showed now, floating ethereally on the ocean of vapour.

On he went, pace after pace, each a labour, as the ground sucked at him, trying to pull him down into the mire. Water, below the moss, plashed at his footfall. Peat hags and white drifts of wind moved canna-bawn went on and on, seemingly without end, as he stumbled over the great tract of land, pathless and untrodden, save by deer; ----- acre upon acre.

In his head a voice kept urging him to stop, to rest, to lay the wounded man down. "Sleep, lie down", said the voice. Great the weariness on him, striving to overcome him. In his mind he fought it, but it would not go away. Now, every scintilla of energy had been stripped from his being.

Tearlach Og's breathing was shallow, with, every now and then, a series of shuddering gasps, his eyes half opening, showing two tiny white half moons. Bleeding had started again and his yellow shirt had turned a dark, ugly, sodden red, where his life-blood oozed out.

Raise the foot, take the step, raise the foot, make the step. Now, it needed a supreme effort of will for his body to comply. His muscles were cramping. He sat down, with the wounded man still on his back, and fell instantly asleep. How long he dozed he could not tell, but, when he awoke, at once he staggered up and again went on. His biceps, his forearms, shoulders, his spine screamed at him; the pain unspeakable. A great shroud of weariness was overcoming him. He lay down and dozed, moving in and out of sleep. Dream fragments filled his mind. Sleep beckoned, but from somewhere he managed to find the strength of will to resist it.

Again he arose. "Just the once. Go on, go on." Now he was staggering, moving, oh so slowly, like a drunken man. It was as if all of the colours of the World had been leached out. There was only whiteness, ghostly, pale and wan, as if life itself had ebbed and washed away his spirit, and in doing so had left him neither sorrow nor hope.

There was no certainty that the wounded man still lived, but he could not set him down, for he knew that if he ever did so, there was no way he could lift him on to his back again. There came a feather of breath, a whisper of sound, slighter than the twitch of a moth's wing; he thought it was Tearlach's, hoped it was Tearlach's?

Then he saw it ------------The Shepherd, away in the far

5

distance, indistinct, its feet shrouded in mist, beautiful as a mountain seen in dreams,-------------- Buachaille Etive Mhor, the gaurdian at the mouth of Glencoe. Straightways, renewed energy flowed into him. He was weary but his resolve strengthened and he went on.

Near Dubh Lochan, beneath the cliffs of Creag Dhubh they found MacIain with Tearlach. Iain the Chief's elder son and young Achtriachtan were amongst them. Bran and Luath his deer hounds, were first; at once they were on their master, licking him and whimpering in joy, as only dogs can do. They'd brought two garrons with them, but it was obvious, that, to put Tearlach Og on a horse was to ask for trouble, so, with gentleness they placed him on a stretcher, and, turn and turn about, four men bore him. They all knew that he was in bad case, near to death, but they also knew that Beaton would, in all probability, be waiting, at The Meeting of the Three Waters, and if Tearlach was still alive, then Beaton was his best chance of a subsequent recovery. For he was a physician without peer.

II. The Conventicle.

Without doubt it had been one of the most exciting days she had ever known, and the most disturbing. She remembered well the time when her Uncle Tam had taken her to the Conventicle. Memories of which came flooding back. Of how they had tramped up into the hills, by way of the Black Water of Dee, which, after rain, ran brown with mud and was flecked with foam. Wet and heavy the roads, but the air was perfumed with mint and bog myrtle. Everything was refreshed, yet the hillsides stood silent and expectant. People had come from every airt; down from the hills; wending through the valleys; from quiet farm- houses in lonely straths and the solitary shielings on the upland moors. Many had travelled far for the service. Some in two wheeled carts, other had come on horseback, but most on foot. Men had been placed, all around, as sentries, armed, with swords, near to hand, driven point down into the turf. Their eyes were never still, sweeping the land, on the lookout for the enemies of the Lord, the dragoons. Never before had Jean seen so many people gathered at one time. Eventually there was upward of four thousand. All around was the murmur of conversation. Suddenly it had stopped ----------- utter silence fell, broken only by the yittering calls of curlews, uluating out across the land --------------- Peden the Prophet came, the most revered of all of the Field Preachers. Two men had lifted him up and placed him on his pulpit, a huge block of whinstone. He had stood above the assembly, clothed in an ample black gown, with white bands at his neck. All eyes had been on him, he, the man who had had miraculous escape, after escape, from the troops who hunted him ----------------- The Chosen of God. He gave the verses of the rhymed psalm that was to be sung,– "The bloody and deceitful man shall not live out half his days", following which the Precentor led off the singing, which rose into the heavens.Peden had taken the Holy Book and kissed it, reading to them the Word, of how Gideon, when called upon by the Lord, had said that "he was the least in his father's house".And the Lord said unto him, "Surely, I will be with thee, and thou shall smite the Midianites as one man"."And the Lord delivered the Midianites into the hand of Gideon, and he smote them and beat down the Tower of Penuel and slew the men of the city, and gave the people of Israel forty years of peace".Again they had prayed and once more sung a psalm asking God for deliverance from their enemies.Silence fell, the air had become charged with expectation, for the principal part of the service was about to begin.Peden lifted his arms and spread them to their full extent; he stood above them, crucified against the void of Heaven, his eyes upraised, seeing beyond the congregation. He was with them in person, but communing with the Almighty, whilst the blood coursed through his veins, filling him with that burning ecstasy which is given only to the true zealot to know."The Lord God shall deliver all thy enemies to thee and thou shall smite them .and utterly destroy them. His sons and all of his tribe. Thou will take all of his towns and utterly destroy the men, and the women, and the little children".For two hours he had harangued them, inveighing against the House of Stewart, and thundering out the message that the Episcopal Office was destitute of Divine Authority. With Biblical references he had pronounced an anathema against the giver and the receiver of Bishopry. He had called down James the Sixth's Declaration that the King was above the Law, and, that, obedience of the people was to him, the King, as God's Lieutenant on Earth, and that, the principal part of a King's mission was to rule by Divine Right."Christ lives and rules alone in His Church, and has given no head-ship, over it, to any Pope, King or parliament, whatsoever. We have no King but Christ".For the first time he had looked at those gathered. Each had felt the touch of his eyes; his, the soul that entered into theirs. Truly, they felt within themselves, he knew those who had sinned.With calm, dispassionate statement he had laid the truth upon them, then he had turned to the moving of their minds by fear; marshalling his arguments, overwhelming the sinner with the drum roll of denunciation. Argument after argument poured from him, in sheets of sound.All had felt awe. Like the storm his vehemence had swept past, and, in the following calm, the clear light of hope had shone on them. The sermon ended; the meaning of its message, to each, his own. Some had been moved by reason, others touched by fear, and yet again others had been inspired by hope; but most of all they had been enspelled by the earnestness of the preacher; bathed in the solemn conviction of the spirit which he had poured forth on them.There had been a last prayer, short and sharp, the last psalm and the final grace of Peden's benediction. Slowly the congregation had melted away, a faint breeze stirring over it. Last to leave had been the sentries. A few had lingered, but the majority had left, knowing the wisdom of dispersing before the Government sodgers appeared. Stillness had stolen in, and, once more, the place of the Conventicle had become an empty bowl among the hills, where the wind had play, and the sound of running water mingled with the cries of upland birds. Once again it was the place of the sheep, but those who had been there knew that it was a place of God. Jean, in her mind, could still see Peden's eyes, blazing white with the Lord's fury.

III. THE CHURCH.

Without doubt he was the best looking man Jean had ever seen. Well built, savagely handsome, of truly noble aspect, with a high forehead; hair, black as obsidian, which had been twined into ringlets, each weighted, to hang straight, with tiny twists of lead. Under dark brows, his beautiful eyes, shone grey and piercing, the most fascinating eyes she had ever looked upon, the colour of late dawn, filled with curiosity and intelligence.   But, this day, that had been something else. -----------   By order of the Privy Council, and at Claverhouse's behest, all of the people of the Sheriffdom of Wigton, Dumfries, Annandale and Kirkcubright, had to attend, at a specified church, in each parish, to be accounted for and to show compliance to the Privy Council's will, also to be told what the Government expected of them. Few there were who did not appear, for the penalties for absence could be severe. Many, however, came principally out of curiosity ----------- --- for a sight of "Bluidy Clavers" himself; the man their clergy had taught them to abhor and hate, whom, week after week, they had castigated and called down before the wrath of God, and derided unto the depths of very Hell. It had been rumoured that he, himself, would be in attendance at Laurieston Kirk. There was the usual hum of conversation. Sunlight shafted through the window in the west wall turning to gold the tiny motes of dust, which hung suspended in the air. Some six hundred were gathered, every pew packed to overflowing. In places people stood in the aisles. Claverhouse entered accompanied by two of his officers, his troopers remaining outdoors. They were dressed in field grey, with the high black bucket topped boots of cavalry men. There was no mistaking who was Claverhouse; he was charismatic and magnetic, exquisitely dressed, with the narrow horseman's hip, his boots polished to a mirror finish. They walked to the front of the altar, where a small table had been set up, with three chairs. Nonchalantly, Claverhouse took the centre one; an officer seated himself on either hand. They called the roll, assiduously noting who were there, those absent, and any present that had not been previously listed. Then the minister began the service.   Little of the religious ceremony was given much consideration by Jean. She, like most of the Congregation, especially the women, spent the time in surreptitiously viewing Claverhouse from the corner of their eyes.Finally, the service was over. Claverhouse rose to address all gathered, thanked them for their attendance, explained to them that before all else their allegiance was to the King, and dismissed them to go about their lawful business On the church steps Claverhouse lingered talking to the minister, who seemed to be uneasy, to be so engaged, as well he might, for there were those who would undoubtedly think that he should have had no truck with such a man. Converse being over he reached out and effortlessly swung up into the saddle of the mare, which had been brought for him. Horses bucked and danced, amidst a gallant clatter of hooves as, with no more ado, the cavalcade moved off. High on a yew tree, in the churchyard, from the top most twig, a thrush sang, full throated, the song ringing out, clearly, over the countryside, with a vibrant rush of notes, which quivered at their core, travelling, in liquid sound, far out over the land .

Before she fell asleep that night Jean thought on Claverhouse. She remembered that the ministers, at the Conventicles, had warned, time and again, that the Devil came in many disguises; that, she must think on, ------ even a few evil thoughts could drag one down into the depth of the pit of unspeakable depravity. Just before sleep the thought occurred to her that, "perhaps, he was The Snake of all of the serpents, the Devil himself, or brother to the Great Lucifer?" But, not withstanding, he was a bonny, bonny man. Dreamless she slept.

IV. CARSECREUGH

Claverhouse cantered up to the front of the House of Carscreugh, accompanied by a small detatchment of Troopers. It was an imposing house, not for its beauty, but for the fact that it was built, by its designer, to be totally remote, a mansion set amidst bleak moorland, a land from which, it appeared, all life had fled, and from which the colours of nature had been leached out over many centuries. It had the feel of timelessness, of solidarity, and mixed it subtly with a grace and finesse of line. The sky was dull and overcast. From far away a curlew piped its pibroch of wild sound. Out beyond, the sea lay, a sheet of grey, with white at the edges, where it met the land. A powerfully muscled hound ran from behind the house barking furiously to warn them off, causing the horses, instantly, to become mettlesome and skittish. With practiced skill Claverhouse dismounted holding out his gloved hand to the dog, addressing it in low tones. Its lips drew back to show its fangs, growling in threat, they remained exposed whilst the expression changed almost to one of smile, its tail began to wag when the hand reached out to fondle its ears.

"I see you have managed to befriend Brutus", said one of the two men who approached. One was taller than the other. That they were father and son, there could be no doubt of, for the family resemblance was strong. Of the two, the son, at once, took Claverhouse's attention, an immaculate man of middle build, dressed in the black and grey of the legal profession with white linen at his throat. Instantly, in the soldier's mind arose the notional image of a magpie, which was heightened by the hard unblinking stare of one who takes stock of what he sees, judges it accordingly, and sifts out that which is to his advantage alone. There was in him that which was unfathomable. His general mien was puritanical; suggesting that he would admit to no margin of error. He had an interesting face with deceptively hooded eyes, quick and sharp as steel. A strange remote man, but, one never to be underestimated; perhaps, never to be trusted. There was a mysterious, dark quality about him, saturnine or satanic, with the coldest eyes Claverhouse had ever seen, except on a snake. The father seemed more self assured, which he had every right to be, being universally acknowledged as the foremost legal intellect in the land, even, as many averred, the greatest lawyer Scotland had ever produced. So, these were the Dalrymples, wrapped about in the mantle of the law, risen by virtue of the booming growth of the legal profession, occasioned by the proliferation of legislation from Parliament and the increase use of litigation by the landed gentry.

"Gentlemen, as Commander of Troops, I call upon you, out of courtesy and to bring word of the requirements of the Privy Council on the keeping of order in this area. There are matters which I must touch on which might best be discussed in private?" The question hung in the air, enigmatically.

"Come, let us adjourn to the house, I will send a servant out with pots of ale for your men".

Within, the house had an air of wealth, yet was strangely stark, reminiscent, to Claverhouse, of the Calvanistic interiors of many of the Dutch mansions he had seen.

"You will take a glass of claret?" the father enquired.

When it was brought the wine, when poured, was jewel bright and fragrant.

With the abruptness of one cross-examining in a Court of Law the son rapped out the question, "What might it be that you wish to talk on?"

Calmly Claverhouse appraised him. "Gentlemen, I have to inform you that, by order of the Privy Council, the House of Carscreugh is to be made available to me for use as a garrison, as, and, when I should so require. It may be incumbent upon you, at times to provide shelter and accommodation for troops and to stable their horses. All food and any hay consumed you will be reimbursed for, by the Government, against bills presented and countersigned by myself".

"You no doubt have a copy of the Order for us?" enquired the elder Dalrymple.

"Indeed, yes", said as he proffered it.

Quickly, Dalrymple scanned it.

Neither of the two men seemed, in any way surprised. Claverhouse surmised that they had already been forewarned, for they had friends in high places, with fast and efficient lines of communication straight from Edinburgh. Frequently, they would have news, from the Capital, more swiftly than he could have it in the field.

"May I keep this? ", asked the father, with a note of asperity in his voice.

"Indeed you may".

"I trust that, should such a need arise, you will do me the courtesy of serving a week's notice of such requirement, also I would hold you personally responsible for any damage which might occur".

. In his mind Claverhouse knew that these men, the most powerful lairds in this part of the country, were rebels. Indeed, he had recently had intelligence that the elder Dalrymple's wife had entertained the infamous Peden, The Prophet, in this very house.

With this in mind Claverhouse was in no mood to indulge in pleasantries. "You may rest assured that any troops, who have occasion to be billeted here, will be under my rule of discipline and as such are unlikely to cause you any problems. I would stress to you, that it would be best, that you should have a care and be on your guard, for rebels abound in this part of His Majesty's Country, and I, and those responsible for apprehending them or rooting them out, will do so with all the force of the law".

"Sire, you have made your position perfectly clear and I would call on you now to leave". There was a distinct note of acerbity, verging on the vitriolic, in the younger Dalrymple's tone of voice.

At once Claverhouse spun on his heel and was out of the door and on his horse. Troopers put down their ale pots and ran for their mounts, to speed after their leader, as he spurred away.

Later, in the week, Sir James, in high dudgeon, wrote to the Marquis of Queensberry, a relative, though of no great closeness.

"It grieved me that a thirty four year old Captain of Horse should have thought fit to take upon himself the proffering of advice to me, the Lord President. My Lord Marquis, as you are aware, I and my son, James, have seen that justice has been administered in Galloway and Glenluce. It does not seem fitting that a mere soldier should deign to instruct me, after all the years of service I have given the State, as to how to conduct myself. As you are aware I have recently been in correspondence with the King and also the Duke of York, with regard to policy. Should you be in a position to perhaps draw to either of their attentions the conduct of the Captain, towards myself, I would deem it a particular favour".

For reasons best known to himself the Marquis chose to ignore Sir James's letter. Perhaps, he deliberately did so, or, perhaps, the pressures of his high political position prevented him replying.

V. MARY

Water fell in beauty, in a thousand silver strings. In the night there had been thunder rain, which had gathered on the tops, unabsorbed by the impervious, fire formed rock, until the burns were in roaring spate and spilled their waters, down the cliffs, to become tendrils of floating silver lace, which, in turn, were teased by the wind into moving curtains, with here and there, the magic of a drifting rainbow; each unique, ephemeral and transient, evanescent as flame.

All of her life she had spent in the presence of mountains, in the trench of the Great Glen or looking out over the lands of Keppoch to the brooding mass of Ben Nevis, but to live in Glencoe was to be of mountains. There was no escape from them, everywhere they overbore you. Their ageless spirits lurked in the gullies, and sang in the rocks, as they ran, never to be caught. She remembered, before she had ever been in Glencoe, that MacIain, before they were wed, had told her of the hold the place could take on one; now she knew. Here was a bittersweet place, ageless as time,

On her way up to Achtriotachan she had passed by Sgor nan Fiannaidh with the great scar on it of the Devil's sword slash, Clachaig Gully, running from the top of its skull to the very edge of its jaw. It was April now and in the depths of the recess ravens sat on eggs and, where there were good deposits of soil, great swags of yellow primroses grew.

As she came over the lip of terminal moraine a flight of Swans flew over her head, which pleased her, for her husband had told her, years before, that luck was given to those that lay in the shadow of their wings. Now she was in the Place of the Yellow Nosed Swans, Loch Achtriotachan. For there, they came, eight to twelve of them, every year, to over-winter. Not like orange nosed Mutes, to be silent,

16

but to speak their minds, honking and calling, all the while; beautiful and white, wild and free, with the yellow of sulphur on their beaks. Soon, very soon, they would leave to spend their summer in the far to the north.

Her day was busy with all of the things that she and Achtriotachan's wife found to do; the swapping of recipes, the mending of clothes, the continuation of the tapestries they had been working on, and in particular the giving of news, each to the other. Over the years, Mary had come to value Achtriotachans' wife's friendship greatly, and they had become very close.

Now, it was time to be off home before darkness came. Mary mounted her pony and set off down the Glen. It was one of those rare days when the wind was almost still. She looked out over the Loch, which lay, unruffled, like a sheet of green glass. Awe took her, for here, in the deep cut of the Glen, she was filled with a sense of wonder. Above all the great wall of Anoach Eagach rose, stark, black, overpowering, a rearing cliff of impervious rock, with fans of scree, delicately worked; a mountain like no other, truly elemental. It was a scene of breathtaking grandeur, a monument to Nature, hewn by the chisels of time. For all of the world she felt that she was in a cathedral. The sense of awe, she felt, would have been just as great, but it would have come from the wonder of a man made thing; here, in the Glen, it was a creation of Nature, which, she knew could not be matched. There was no great canvas of colours, only the black of igneous rock, and the filigrees of scree, the silver of falling water, the infinite greens of plants, which had struggled to live, and to continue to live, for thousands of years; all of it melded to please the eye, to bring balm to the soul.

It was an hour and a half after she had returned when MacIain came home from Carnoch, where he had been about some Clan business.

First he saw to it that his deerhounds, Luath, Bran, and Griane were fed.

"How was your day?" he asked, as he stripped off his sword and took the blunderbuss from his back.

"One of the best I ever had, she replied.

Mary told him of the magic of the swans and the spell of Achtriochatan. And both were content in the happiness of each other.

VI. LUCE.

Here and there the corn had just begun to yellow as Claverhouse's brother led his detail of troopers, as commanded, up to Lochlands House. The sky was overcast with a cold wind blowing in off the sea. There was an air of desolation about the place; no dog barked, no poultry scraped a living from the earth, no smoke rose from the chimneys of the dwelling. Disturbed, crows rose in a mighty calling throng, beating across the sky, in a discordant clamour. As had been expected the House had been deserted. Nevertheless, the soldiers knew what they had to do, to seize and take off any goods they could find, from this rebel laird, the tenant of Sir John Dalrymple. With practised skill they searched the house and every out-building. Little did they find, but still, it was sufficient to fill a cart, which they'd brought along with them. There was a serviceable plough, a milk churn, a bushel-measure, bit and pieces of harness, several replacement horseshoes, a pair of oak chests and a table with heavily carved legs. There was no livestock, though, eventually, they did come upon a dog kennel, which they also loaded on to their wagon.

Last of all they nailed a notice, on the front door of the house, which informed anyone who chose to read it, that, by order of the Privy Council," This house, out buildings, plenishings, live stock and any posessions, of the laird, thereof, were forfeit, as was becumbent upon those in rebellion on the Government" A footnote informed all and sundry that anyone offering succor to the Laird would also be held to be in rebellion.

Furious at this interference Sir John Dalrymple expostulated with the Privy Council, as to Claverhouse's meddling with his tenants.

A letter was delivered, to Claverhouse, from Sir John, Demanding to know what he was about in seizing, for the Crown, rebel goods that should have been his?

In response, Claverhouse, confident as to his rights as Sheriff, ordered that a message should be read from the pulpit of Glenluce Church, summoning the local people to attend a court hearing of the affair, and, at which, a head count would be taken.

On the appointed day Claverhouse rode with ten troopers to town, for the hearing. As they clattered up the street there was a stillness in the air, even the wind seemed paused, though the rain came down hard. All were sopping wet, the horses and the men, even though they wore their military rain proofs. There were few people about. Any they saw seemed to be young lads, there were no adults. With a growing sense of uneasy expectancy Claverhouse dismounted and strode towards the Town House door. At his command his men remained in the saddle, readying their carbines.

At Claverhouse's push the door swung inwards. Within were only two persons, the Dalrymples, father and son.

"Where are all of the populace summoned to appear?" enquired Claverhouse.

"It would seem they were unable to come, for some reason or other" replied the elder Dalrymple. "Perhaps the rain put them off?" In the air the question hung, enigmatic, full of transient, quizzical irony.

"You, sirs, are at the back of this", thundered Claverhouse, in anger. His voice reverberating in the empty space.

There was a pregnant pause, in which neither of the Dalrymples spoke.

"Then, maybe, that is for the best ", said Sir James. "For we wished to talk with you alone."

" Pray Sirs, speak your minds, for I would most certainly like to know what is afoot. You, Sirs, are responsible for the non-attendance of the people I know, for the bulk of them are your tenants. Is that not so?"

Sir John, immaculate as ever, in his dark suit, replied. "There are affairs, in this part of the world, that are best left to the military, and things of justice and jurisprudence, which are best left to those of the law, who have steered the populace in the past, and who are the appointed legal upholders of the Offices of the Law. That there are trouble makers and rabble-rousers abroad no one can deny, but these will be brought to face the court, by the military, as required, and then be sentenced by the law. This, you will agree."

Claverhouse, at once, was aware of what they were about. He knew that, above all, despite the anger he felt, he must remain calm, on all counts, for, these two men were the most powerful lairds in the south west, and were, without doubt, two of the sharpest legal minds in the land, and, perhaps, most important of all, they had friends of influence, in high places.

"Gentlemen, I would draw to your attention the fact that I am under the orders of the Privy Council, who have invested me with the military command over Galloway, Nithsdale and Dumfries, and have seen fit to appoint me, as Sheriff, over the said lands. Which gives me, also, the legal right to apprehend rebels, law breakers and wrongdoers, to try them and award the necessary punishment, as required."

Silence hung on the air. There was a pause of perhaps a minute, when no one spoke.

Arising from his pew, Sir John spoke in his sonorous voice, which, with years of practice, he had learnt to pitch to suit his audience. "Knowing of your circumstances, wherin you are called upon to find the wherewithall to provide uniforms for your men and fodder for your horses, and that the Privy Council are often tardy in forwarding funds to you, we are of the opinion that the circumstances could be ameliorated, with perhaps a surplus being available to yourself?" The silence hung in the air, the pause trembling enigmatically, with both parties hoping for an outcome favourable to themselves." My son and I have in mind the sum of one hundred and fifty pounds, to make up the loss of revenues you would incur by being deprived of the Glenluce fines."

Thunderstruck, Claverhouse's mind raced. Such a sum, enough to feed and clothe his men for at least three years, with a handsome residue for himself; money indeed.

"You would offer to me, the Military Authority in these lands, what I would deem to call a bribe, a considerable sum of money. In return I expect, that you would wish me to allow you to continue to be the arm of the Law, in this quarter, unhindered, unopposed; indeed, for you to continue as before?"

Sir John coughed; his throat cleared he addressed Claverhouse. "Should you have reservations as to the sum offered or wish to discuss any aspects of a mutually beneficial arrangement, we would be pleased to enter into a compact suitable to each party"

With alacrity Claverhouse rose from his bench, drawing himself up to his full height. With the thunder of a cannon he spoke. "Never have I been so affronted. Never have I heard of so despicable a suggestion. I tell you now I will have no truck with your low ploy. Now I see why you wanted to speak with me alone. No taint of corruption will touch me". At that, he stormed out of the building, mounted his horse and rode off at the gallop, his troopers straggling behind, splashing through the puddles, whilst the rain continued to fall with unremitting ferocity.

In view of what had transpired, Sir John, at once, hurried to Edinburgh to get his word in first, before this upstart soldier presented his report. There were those, on the Privy Council, who had no love for Claverhouse, in particular Hamilton. Convinced that his case was sound Dalrymple accused Claverhouse of oppressing and laying waste the countryside, of permitting the troops to act lawlessly, and asked for Graham to be recalled. He was stunned to be told that the Council was in full approval of what Claverhouse was about in Galloway. Queensberry, in turn, as Secretary of State, also concurred with the Council, even though he was distantly related to the Dalrymples, for he knew that in matters pertaining to their personal affairs they could prove to be over sensitive and mettlesome.

On his return from Edinburgh father and son met to discuss the situation. They were still of the opinion that the Council had not fully considered all of the points they had made, so, with there undoubted, superior, knowledge of the law, they searched for ways to circumvent Graham's authority.

"I have it, " said Sir James, after pondering on the Course of action to follow. "Supplementary Sheriffs are commissioned to try "First Attachers", that is, persons who have not yet been prosecuted. There are many who have been questioned by Claverhouse, who were found guilty, but were put on probation, before being brought to decisive trial. Therefore, we should call a Regality Court, at which we should pass judgement on these people".

"Father, the simplicity of it all is sublime. You have come up with a scheme, which is, in my opinion, perfect". With that both men quaffed the remains of the claret in their glasses. Again, Sir John reflected, who has better knowledge of the law, who can put it to better use than my father? "Let's drink to that". So, they called on their servant to bring another bottle of the best.

In August, Sir John called his Regality Court, tried the "Attachers" and fined them derisory catchpenny amounts. Thereby, removing them, as "First Attachers", from Graham's hands. Now, that they had been dealt with, there was no further action, the Dalrymples could see, that Claverhouse, in law, could pursue.

They rubbed their hands, warmed by the knowledge that, with their superior grasp of legalities, they had outwitted this louche loup–the–dyke, whom the Privy Council had seen fit to foist upon them.

The response of Graham was swift and vexatious. Peremptorily, he arrested most of the Dalrymples' chief tenants, including one of Sir James's right hand men----- his Factor, and nearly all of the officials of the Regality Court. The charges levelled at them were that they had been attending conventicles and had been absent from their parish churches. In all the fines imposed on them, to the fullest range of Claverhouse's powers, came to in excess of one thousand pounds, an unheard of sum.

In view of the fact that the sums levied were beyond any of their means, they were committed to prison. Also, in order to prevent the Stairs stirring up further trouble Graham had an announcement made, in every church in Galloway, that whomsoever had any complaint against his troops should present it, at Strathaven, to the persons, duly appointed, who would give them satisfaction, should any submission prove to be justified. David, Grahams' brother, was given the job and he seemed to carry it out to the reconciliation of most parties.

A galloper came, post haste from Strathaven. His horse was fatigued, but not yet at the stage of foundering. At once, the Sergeant of the Guard had the rider taken to the room, in Dumfries Castle, which Claverhouse used as his office, for the Sergeant knew that the dispatch he carried must be of importance.

With promptness Graham arose from behind his desk. He immediately took in the fact that the trooper was weary and must have ridden long and hard. " Leave me the dispatch you bring, go see to your horse and see that the cook feeds you".

Filled with interest Graham slit the document open. It was from his brother.

'Dear John', it read. ' I send this, post haste, by my best galloper, Ferguson, whom I know will have driven his mount hard, but, at all times, with regard to its welfare. What I have to report is, in my judgement, of importance, and I knew you would wish to have word of it at the earliest'.

Filled with interest Claverhouse began to read what was a deposition, handed in, in person, by Sir John's agent, Samuel MacAdam, which purported to be the protest of all of the heritors of Glenluce. In short it complained of their treatment by the military, both officers and men.

Later, knowing that Ferguson would have eaten, Claverhouse sent for him.

The trooper saluted.

"Be seated", said his Commander.

Ferguson was nonplussed, for no officer had ever asked him to sit before.

"Sit ye doon man. Your officer, at Strathaven, speaks highly of you, You have done well, which will be noted. What you have brought me requires consideration, in which case the response, which you alone will carry back, will not be ready for two days. Therefore, you are excused all duties, until, you report back to me, at eight o'clock on Wednesday morning ".

Despite his tiredness, Ferguson rose, saluted smartly, and marched from the room.

Knowing that speed was his best weapon Claverhouse pondered deeply as to how best to make the next move in the campaign against the Dalrymples. He slept little in the next forty-eight hours, cognisant of the fact, that, in knowledge of the law, he was a child in comparison to his adversaries. Nevertheless, his was the military command of the south- west, and his was the Office of Sheriff, by the appointment of the Privy Council, the supreme authority in the land, save the King. Buoyed by this he resolved on his course of action.

On the Wednesday morning the galloper was sent north, to Strathaven, with the reply to Graham's brother, with instructions to 'not hurry, as there was no need for haste'. David was informed that notices should be posted in every town, in Claverhouse's jurisdiction, and that from every pulpit in the churches, in the said bounds, the populace should be informed that Claverhouse would preside at the Court, in Strathaven, a week hence. All, from the lands listed, were eligible to attend

There was heat in the air, though the day was still young, and there was a bustle about, much more than usual, in this normally douce town. As the troops rounded the base of the Castle, jackdaws called, cawing one to the other as they flew about their business. Horse hooves pounded on the brick hard ground as the file of soldiers rode down the wide main street. Chimmneys gave off black smoke as housewives prepared their breakfasts, but it seemed that any food being cooked would be for women and children only, for all of the male population of the town appeared to be abroad, in particular, thronged around the Court House.

At a barked command every trooper dismounted, each making his way to an allotted position, to instructions previously given; some remaining outside, with muskets to hand, whilst others, unarmed, went inside.

Accompanied by his brother and two other officers Claverhouse entered. There was not a vacant seat to be seen and every aisle was jam-packed with standing people. The press of the crowd was very great.

To bring order, Claverhouse rapped on the table with his gavel. A hush fell.

"This Court of the Sheriff, John Graham, duly appointed by the Privy Council, is now convened", intoned one of the officers." It will hear any complaints brought against the conduct of any of the military, whether it be in the matter of the quartering of troops, of the provision of fodder for horse, or of any seemed injustice suffered by the appellants".

There was a stramash at the door. As one, every head turned to see what was afoot. None could have been more surprised than Graham, for, immaculate as ever, Sir John Dalrymple burst in, despite the attentions of two soldiers. In haste, filled with purpose, he made his way towards the bench, seating himself on the only vacant chair.

Nonplussed, Claverhouse remained silent, though his eyebrows rose in question.

"As Hereditary Sheriff I will preside over the proceedings, as empowered".

With one of the quick, instinctive flashes, of which he was, later, to be remembered for, it dawned upon Graham as to how he could use this wholly unexpected intervention to his advantage. "Let the deposition laid by Samuel MacAdam be read out in full, in which accusations were made in general, but not in particular, against the military. Thereafter, once it has been read, I will hear from any man present his complaint, which will be dealt with without fear or favour".

Silence fell, in which was only heard the buzzing of bluebottles, high up in the rafters, and the occasional scuff of feet. Time drew on seemingly interminably.

"Has no man here a word to say?" asked Graham.

Sir John rose placing both his palms on the table. In anger he spoke, his words reverberating in the chamber, thundering out. "Who are the army to come into lands which had no need of them? Who are they to molest the populace? Who are they to requisition hay for their horses, and the value of it to go unpaid for? Is it not the case that, in this very town, a man, about his lawful business, perfectly innocent, was wounded by a musket shot? Has not this John of Claverhouse broken the law for his own ends?" For a brief moment he paused, then he began again. "Has he not put to his own use fines levied? In which case, I, the Heritable Sheriff, will make him pay for it". Finished for the moment, thought obviously in a state of high dudgeon, the lawyer subsided back on to his seat.

Claverhouse, in turn, rose, took a few steps, clasped his hands behind his back and addressed the gathering. There was no hint of anger in his voice, though within he seethed. "First, let us address the matter of import, before we move on to the much less pressing accusations levelled by this Interloper" Whom he indicated by a nod of his black haired bewigged-head, and the obvious sarcasm placed on the word Interloper.

Again, Sir John was on his feet. "This is an affr----------------
-------------". He got no further.

"Sir, you will address this Court as and when you are called upon, not when you so wish. You will remain silent until I, the Sheriff, as commissioned by the Privy Council, the foremost authority, after the King, permit you to speak. First, as previously stated, the matter of prime importance to all of the lawful citizens gathered here will be given due consideration. Speak out any of you, who so wish, any of you who have complaint".

No one raised his voice. No arm was raised to draw attention. No seated person rose.

"In which case, I take it, there being no word or accusation against the forces of the King, none have a wish to proceed with any of the scurrilous or fabricated charges brought by Samuel MacAdam. Therefore I find them all to be false".

Again Dalrymple leapt to his feet. With no request, to the Court, to be permitted to speak, he began. "You, Sirah, are a damnable upstart, a tool of men whom though they, themselves, sit on the Privy Council, are corrupt selfseekers and are --------------".

As at one, two of the troopers, near to hand, at Claverhouse's indication seized hold of the lawyer, who was incandescent, his face livid purple totally suffused with blood, rage boiling in him, invective spewing from him, lowered to the level of the kailyard. With an ease, which spoke of drill square practice, each trooper took an arm, gripped it and then proceeded to draw Sir John along the central aisle, out of the building, with his body held at an angle of thirty degrees, the heels of his boots leaving two black scores along the wood panelled floor. For a lawyer to have been bested by a soldier was bad enough, but to have been made out to be a liar, before all, and having been manhandled in such an unseemly manner was mortifying, simply beyond all bearing.

Talk that night in the alehouses was all of the Court proceedings. Generally, it was agreed that there had never before been such entertainment in the head courts of Galloway and Dumfries.

Taking cognisance of what had occurred at the Court at

26

Strathaven, and having considered all of the facts, the Privy Council sent a note to the Dalrymples as to how Heritable Bailies or Sheriffs should not offer to compete with any appointed by the Council.

Perturbed and shaken by the unexpected turn of events the Dalrymple family, taking a leaf out of the Clans Chiefs' book, decided that discretion, and the spreading of risk to their family fortune and estates, would be the better part of valour. As a first step, they sent their womenfolk abroad, and, in particular Sir James's wife, a rabid Presbyterian, and one suspected of having given succour and accommodation to Scotland's most wanted man, the infamous preacher Peden. They were to be installed, into Dutch society, by Argyll, The Chief of Clan Campbell, who had previously fled to be with William of Orange.

Very shortly afterwards Sir James followed to be with Argyll, his erstwhile pupil. His was the realisation that, soon, he would be called upon to take the Test, the Act, the drawing up of which, he had been largely responsible, wherein persons were called upon to swear solemn allegiance to the Monarch. This, in all conscience, he knew, he could not do.

In Edinburgh, making arrangements to have fresh supplies of powder, from the Cannonmills, sent to his troops, and to have some new uniforms made up for the men, Claverhouse took the opportunity to socialise with his good friend the Duke of York. On several occasions they met in one of the new and fashionable coffee-houses in the High Street. Usually these were packed to overflowing, for here the gentry and the affluent merchants and those in high command in the navy or the armed forces met, to exchange views, to strike bargains, or simply to enjoy the fellowship of friends. Or, perhaps, to say that they had seen the Duke of York, or better still had bidden him 'Good Morning'. Or, even better than that, that He had exchanged words with them.

Once or twice the Duke took Graham along to the links, at Leith, to play golf. But Claverhouse could never quite take to the game. Perhaps the lack of pace, as they strolled round hitting the ball, or, in his case, the apparent inability to strike the feathered missile away into the far distance, was, if he was honest, such a frustration as to make enjoyment nearly an impossibility. And, if one watched the partner James Duke of York frequently played with, John Paterson, a shoemaker, but, renowned at the golf, you were left with the feeling that, if you tried for forty years, you would never be so good or even come so near.

However, Claverhouse found, or had found, in tennis, from the very first game he took part in, that, of all athletic pursuits, this was the one he liked best. Every thing about it appealed to him. There was no sporting sensation so thoroughly enjoyable to him, as that, of which, when he met a tennis ball, in the very middle of his raquet, and smacked it, just right, to the place where his opponent should be, but was not, due to being outfoxed or beaten by the pace or the placing of the ball, there was a crazy excitement, a mad thrill, when it happened 'just right'. There was also the pleasure of tactically beating your opponent. Perhaps, this appealed to the military man in him?

'What delightful paper the invitation was written on, so white, and the ink so golden. With the Ducal Coat of Arms also delineated in gold'.

"His Highness James Duke of York and The Duchess, Mary Beatrice, will be pleased to have the attendance of John Graham of Claverhouse, on the 6th. of September, for the performance of "The Spanish Friar", By the Duke' s Oxford Company of Players, at the Tennis House, adjacent to the Watergate, at eight o'clock of the evening. There will be a reception, afterwards, to which you are invited".

This was a delight indeed. For one thing Claverhouse had never met the Duchess, though he had heard much of her, for Edinburgh had taken her to itself, and conversation centred on her doings and on her person. Indeed, after the Restoration, following the reign of Cromwell, wherein all enjoyments, of any kind, had been suppressed, and the power wielded by the Presbyterian fundamentalists had led to constraints on many things, including the theatre, forward thought and intellectual teachings, sports and many other aspects in every walk of life, the arrival of James Duke of York had been like a breath of fresh air to the vast majority of the people. Already Edinburgh had its own Town Guard, founded by the Duke, for the purpose of keeping law and order. All hundred of them were dressed in rust red and armed with Lochaber axes. The Law had taken on a new lease of life, with the founding of The Advocates Library, in which James showed a great deal of interest. To the north of the town a botanical garden had been laid out for the purpose of producing herbs for use in medicine. Also, The College of Surgeons had been founded, to enhance the standing of its members and to further research and the dissemination of medical knowledge. Down at the port of Leith all was hustle and bustle with expansion taking place. New warehouses were going up, new breakwaters and new docks were under construction. Certainly, since James Duke of York had come north to Edinburgh the town had bloomed.

Always when he came to the Capital Claverhouse felt a frisson of excitement, for here was an atmosphere of wealth, There was always something new, taking place, and, above all you could scent raw power. No where was like the High Street, leading down from the Castle to the Palace of Holyrood, where the rearing houses went up to six and seven stories high, some almost touching, in the air, across the street from each other. Also, there, stood the Town Cross, the Church of St.Giles, and the Tolbooth, where troublemakers were imprisoned.

All was light, hundreds of lanterns flared, carriages came and went, depositing their passengers, sedan chairs arrived borne by liveried porters. At the doorway two of the Town Guard were on duty, tricked out in their rust red uniforms. Guests, as they entered, were questioned by a Major Domo as to their names and relevant ranks and announced accordingly.

On entry all were amazed for the interior had been decorated with foliage of the firtree and countless vases of flowers, which perfectly enhanced the setting.

With courtesy the Duke greeted each arrival introducing them to the Duchess.

"James", she chided, "you told me that he was handsome, but not this handsome".

Embarrassment came to Claverhouse, but he was of sufficient experience to be able to handle it. In turn, he, as were most, was struck by her beauty, as her blonde hair rippled and flamed with white fire in the candlelight. Her gown was all of one fabric, simply cut, in dove grey velvet, which made her skin glow like porcelain. Around her throat she wore a necklace, which had been the present of her husband, of fresh water pearls, from the River Tay; not the lucent white of those raised in sea water, but a lambent silver.

.' How wonderful',Claverhouse mused, is the beauty of the only gem stone which is the fruit of a living creature. But, would it seem so marvellous were it not on the neck of one so fair?'

Despite her Italian inflexion of speech the Duchess spoke excellent English. With unconcealed glee she introduced Graham to her three ladies - in – waiting, who were in attendance, Lady Jean, Lady Mary and Jemima. Pointedly she informed him that he should sit, in the Ducal, box next to Jemima. With surprise he sat not having expected, despite his friendship with the Duke, to be placed with the Duchess only two seats away. He could have done without Jemima for she was young, and though pretty, he had, at once, read her as coquettish. Indeed, as the evening progressed, he did find her so, for much to his discomfit, there were times when her foot found his and he was of the opinion that it was not always by chance. Nevertheless, the play was sublime; it flowed with a professionalism of presentation, the drama crafted to hold all attention. At the interval everyone in the box were served with cordials or, if one chose, a concoction, which James had had brought from London, made by one of that city's 'Strong Watermen', as James put it. After you had drunk it Claverhouse was glad that it had been served in glasses that were tiny, for it was indeed fierce. In fact, that Jemima had had two tots, seemed to make her laughter more frequent and more high pitched, and to have heightened her complexion.

After the play was completed and the Company had received the plaudits of the whole audience there was the Reception for those chosen. In attendance was Collin Lindsay, the Earl of Balcares, whose wife was Claverhouse's second cousin. Lindsay was an old time friend of the Duke, having fought with him at sea, where he had distinguished himself at Solebay: Lord Ross: the formidable General Tam Dalziel; the Earl of Aberdeen: Queensberry: Sir George Mackenzie of Rosehaugh, King,s Advocate, a Dundee man and old friend: the Duke of Hamilton: the Countess of Moray: Lord Doune: a number of retired Lord Provosts of the City: William

Dick, the most prosperous of all Merchant, who had a fleet of seven ships, which sailed to the Baltic, the Mediteranean, and the Low Countries: the Primate of Scotland, with four other churchmen, all clad in black, like so many crows: and the Lord of Glenorchy, whom Graham had never clapped eyes on before. He, the second most powerful member of the Clan Campbell, who had the reputation for being familiar with every political game ever played.

Three days later Claverhouse had news, from his brother, which sent him, post- haste, back to Galloway.

'Certainly, there were things to be missed about Edinburgh, but to be abroad again, on the rolling hills of Galloway, under the great sweep of sky, with his troopers about him was a pleasure indeed', Claverhouse mused. There was much to attend to, work, which had built up in his absence, though he was pleasantly surprised at how smoothly it all had operated, whilst he was away.

Four days later his weekly despatches, from the Capital arrived. With them was a package, a box voluminously wrapped in folds of linen. This, Claverhouse decided, he must open first, before seeing to the instructions of the Privy Council and the military command. Within he found a magnificent pocket watch. Reading the note which accompanied it compounded his delight for it had been sent to him by James Duke of York ------ 'In appreciation of the good works which you carry out for the King. This I have had made for you by Paul Romieu, the French clockmaker, of the West Bow. The case is of silver, won from the King's mine, the God's Blessing'.

It truly was a work of art with his initials, chased into the case in swirling, exquisitely proportioned arabesques, the ends terminating in delicate swags of foliage.

Next, Claverhouse opened a letter, which bore the seal of the Privy Council, but not the usual seal of dispatches of a military order. The contents, of which, struck him like a thunderbolt. 'John Graham of Claverhouse be informed that a Bill of Suspension, against yourself, has been laid before the Council by Sir James and Sir John Dalrymple You are charged with having proceeded illegally, in that the persons fined had already been dealt with by the Heritable Sheriff, who handed down much lighter impositions. Until the Council proceed to consider the Bill, it has been decided to set at liberty all of the tenants previously imprisoned and all fines levied are sequestered. Further, it is alleged that troops were quartered, without payment being made in restitution of the sums due in respect of this. And you, James Graham, appropriated monies, paid from fines, to your on use'.

'What to do?' At once Claverhouse decided to return to the Capital to take legal advice as to how he should proceed.

VII. SALMON.

For hundreds of years the Lairds of Glenorchy had considered that any salmon which ran up from the sea into the Rivers Orchy, Lochy, Strae or Awe, was theirs, and theirs alone. However, there were many, in the Highlands, who believed that a salmon belonged to the man who caught it, as did the fowls of the air and the deer on the hills. Since time immemorial the men of Glencoe had taken the king of fish on this basis, mostly from the prolific River Orchy, particularly in autumn, but, best of all, they savoured the spring run fish, bars of silver, clean run from the sea.

This difference, as to the rights of ownership, had led, on many occasions, to strife between Glenorchy and Glencoe. Sometimes the result had been bloodshed or even to men having been slain, increasing the resentment between the two Clans, so that each had come to look at the slightest insult, given or received, as an affront to the Clan, all of which was compounded by the aversion felt by the Campbells for the MacDonalds and vice versa.

MacIain had sent two men to check on the River Orchy and report on whether or not there had been a run of fish up out of Loch Awe, and, if there had been, whether there was a head of fish in the big holding pool, below the Falls of Chathardh. Word came back that the pool was indeed full, with some fine fish showing.

Without wasting any time, before the next spate came to send water down, to allow the fish to ascend the falls, MacIain made his move. He took fifteen men with him and fifteen garrons, twelve of which, each had a pair of empty panniers slung across its back. The other three horses carried the necessary equipment for the task.

It was carefully timed so that they would arrive in darkness. MacIain knew the moon was only four nights off the full, so, there would be sufficent light. They had come south using every fold of the ground to give them cover. At the river bank, all in silence, each man carried out his allotted task. They stanced the horses, well back, in a clump of trees, then they drove a post into the ground on the north bank, using a cloth to muffle the maul. No one spoke, the only sound was the rush of the falls, which pulsed with life, and on occasion the cry of a night bird. To the post they attached the end of the net they had brought, the other end they roped on to the strongest garron. With care the pony was taken down stream to the tail of the pool, where it was led into the water and then walked across to the other bank, a task which became more difficult with each step, as the unfolding length of the net became greater, offering increased resistance to the flow of water.

MacIain realised that one pony was insufficient and quickly had a further two brought. Once they were yoked the task became easier. Now they tightened the ring of the net in the pool, the garrons being led in an ever decreasing spiral. Salmon began to show, splashing on the surface or leaping clear, the moonlight touching them to silver. Panic stricken fish ran at the net hitting it with great force; the dunt of the larger fish, against it, often causing the ponies to stagger. Now the sounds increased. This was the time at which there was most danger, for, there was no way that the level of noise could be kept down. MacIain trusted that his upstream and downstream sentries would remain vigilant and send word, at sufficient interval, of any alarm, to permit all to melt away. As the net tightened the salmon became more frenzied rushing about and leaping high out of the water. Men were inside the ring now gaffing the fish and despatching them when caught and then carrying them up on to the bank where others loaded them into the ponies' panniers.

In all they took eighty five stone of fish, a truly great haul, with the largest scaling out at thirty two pounds. The men of Glencoe were hugely pleased with their night's work.

Three days later, The Laird of Glenorchy, following a successful day fishing the Pass of Brander, with his guests, Campbell of the Aird, Sir Collin Sheriff of Argyll and MacNaughton of Dunderave, when they had taken, on rod and line, fourteen salmon, brought them "to do some real fishing on the Orchy". For the whole of a long day, with conditions near to perfect for angling, they flogged the water with many changes of flies, the Dipper, the Yellow Dog, Argyll's Fancy, the Cruachan Terror, but they did not touch a fish. Glenorchy was furious, for he knew that the pool had been poached, this, one of his, the best of all. Before his guests he would lose face; his rage ignited, flaring like flame. They saw his anger lines form and knit on his forehead, tendrils of ire webbed in his voice. His guests said nothing, his ghillies were afeared. They knew that, later, they would experience his wrath. His rage boiled, white-hot. There was no proof, but in his heart he knew that his pool had been cleaned out by the men of Glencoe. There could have been others, The Halkit Stirk, the outlaw out of Rannoch, the Magregors, the Fletchers, but his instinct told him that this was the work of MacIain. Everything reeked of MacIain, the planning, and the lack of clues, the very neatness and timing of it all, it could only be down to the Fox of Glencoe. Malice grew in him, and with it his bitterness increased, the bile sour in his throat, for, he was a man who had never come to terms with being thwarted, and, in particular, losing face. He knew it would gnaw at him, a canker in his entrails, until he had brought the perpetrators to heel.

"God damn MacIain".

VIII. PETITIONS.

"In view of all you have informed me of the affair with the Dalrymples, James, it is my considered opinion that, to coin a military phrase, "attack is often the best form of defence". In which case I think we should, in turn, present a Bill of Complaint, to the Privy Council, against the gentlemen in question".Claverhouse. looked at his long time friend, Sir George Mackenzie, the Lord Advocate.

"George, if that is what you think best to do then so be it, for, as a mere soldier, I have neither the knowledge or experience as to how to operate in such circumstances". "Very well, then, we will have the Bill drawn up and presented".

Four days later, the Bill duly formulated to the satisfaction of them both, Claverhouse was once more off to Galloway.

Not since Argyll's trial, thirty years before, had an affair caused such a great stir in the Capital, in the Coffee Houses, at the Privy Council and at the Court of Session. It was indeed the talk of the town. Eminent lawyers took sides. On James Graham's behalf the Kings Advocate wrote to Lord Aberdeen, with the backing of Mackenzie of Tarbat, the Lord Clerk Register.

Others took up the Dalrymples' cause.

Gradually, Claverhouse became concerned, his feeling being that the balance was tilting against him. Alarmed, knowing that trial in open court, often went against all predictions, and, fully conscious of the fact that his career could disappear into nothingness, in desperation, he asked the Council for permission to go to London, to present his case at Court.

The reply was swift. Permission was refused, by order of the Duke of York, for reasons best known to himself. Perhaps, he thought it prudent that his brother, the King, know as little of the affair as possible, or, that, to allow it to pass from Edinburgh to London would undermine his own authority?

Amidst all of the stramash of the hearings, with all of the attendant rumours, proffering of opinions, innuendoes, the giving and taking of bets on the likely outcome, Claverhouse had one great uplift of the spirit. On Christmas Day he was gifted, what his heart had craved for, for years, four troops of horse, to be made into one regiment, to be under the command of Colonel James Graham of Claverhouse. This unit was to be known as "His Majesty's Regiment of Horse". Command of the fourth troop was to be by his cousin's husband, the Earl of Balcarres.

That night, as he sipped a glass of claret and stood looking out of his lodging's window, over the black water of the Nor' Loch, his soul sang. He raised his glass and drank a private toast to' the Duke of York, His Majesty the King, and Mars,'The God of War'.

In all there were three hearings. From the outset it was apparent that neither man could conceal his mutual dislike, both sensed ambition in the other.

Dalrymple, with his supercilious and sarcastic manner, early on angered Claverhouse.

"You Sir are contemptuous and the way in which you express yourself, with regard to myself, is arrogant, overbearing and insolent. Should you continue in this vein I will box your ears".

Like a drum roll, in an instant, the clamour of the hammer of the Chancellor's gavel sounded out. A hush fell, all lapsed into stillness.

" I would remind you, the Complainants, that this is the Court of the Privy Council, and that when any persons appear before it they will do so in a way that is seemly, and they will treat all concerned as gentlemen. The Court will not permit verbal harangues or unfit comments to be made. You will lead arguments or present evidence in a straightforward way without reference to the personality or idiosyncrasies of the parties involved".

Suitably chastened Claverhouse gradually cooled allowing his common sense to overcome his temper. Though, on occasions, as the case proceeded, the Chancellor did raise his eyebrows when either Complainant appeared to be allowing his testimony to become heated or too personal, which gesture seemed to have the necessary calming effect.

Included in the jury of eminent men were The Lord Chancellor, The Primate of All Scotland, The Lord High Treasurer and The Lord Privy Seal.

After the third sitting Claverhouse still felt that the arguments of Dalrymple would prevail and that he would end up as looser. His friend, Sir George Mackenzie was more sanguine, believing that the case they had put forward was sound and would bear more weight. There was an argument, current in the town, which averred that Sir George was worth any two of the lawyers on the otherside, but Claverhouse did not underrate Dalrymple's dextrity of mind, which, coupled with the lawyers representing him, presented a force as potent as any to be found.

In February the Committee met to give judgement.

There was not a single free space in the Court, indeed to accommodate the throng, the partitions which divided the room had been removed. The southern portion, which was the home of the Court of Session now amalgamated with the northern part, which was where the Sheriff Court was held, gave a spacious hall, with a fine oaken roof. Expectation filled the air, the atmosphere throbbed with the anticipation of the outcome. Lawyers who had no connection with the case, politicians, military men, indeed anyone who could get in was there. There was a strong presence of the Town Guard, deployed to keep order.

As the Committee filed in to take their places at the bench the hubbub of conversation stilled. All stood.

The Chancellor opened, informing all that the judgement had been reached in the matter of the Bill of Suspension presented by Sir James Dalrymple, against John Graham of Claverhouse, and the counter Bill of Complaint laid against Sir James, by Claverhouse.

"**One**, you, Sir James have cast aspersions on the man appointed to the military command, in Dumfries and Galloway, by the Privy Council, and who also was appointed as Sheriff of the said area. In view of the complexities of the task and the nature of the designated area to be policed the Council consider that these aspersions are without foundation. It is also our opinion that in casting these calumnies you also have impugned the authority of the Council. **Two,** John Graham is acquitted of any wrong doing, having acted in accordance with the commission given to him, carrying out his duties in such a way as to having fulfilled the trust placed in him, to the great advantage of his Majesty, the King. All charges levelled by Sir John Dalrymple have been found to be not proven to infer any crime against the Military Commander, in which case they are dismissed" At this juncture the Chancellor halted to take a drink of water.

At once the Sound of conversation began, rising to a clamour, as everyone seemed to want to speak to his neighbour, or shout across to some one further off.

With alacrity and full of the sense of his importance the Chancellor beat on his table. Gradually the noise subsided.

"**Three,** Sir John Dalrymple, you are found guilty on all of the charges brought against you. The sentence of this Court is that, firstly, you are stripped of the Sheriffdom of Glenluce. Secondly, You are fined the sum of five hundred pounds and are ordered to pay all costs of this trial. Thirdly, you are committed to be warded, in prison, in the Castle, during the Council's pleasure".

Again, the uproar arose. Unable to contain himself Claverhouse embraced his Counsel. It was more than he could ever have hoped for. Exultation sang through his veins. He turned to look at Dalrymple, but already he had been led off by a detachment of the Town Guard, with their halberds at the high port.

On the twentieth of February Dalrymple was freed from the Castle, at the Council's will, though he was strictly forbidden to leave the bounds of the town of Edinburgh. There were those, in the minority, who considered that the sentence imposed had been too harsh, but that the fine and the loss of the Sheriffdom should stand.

IX. LONDON.

At the start of the year, before the Dalrymple/Claverhouse affair had ceased Edinburgh had been entertained by a scandal of great import, namely the Mint Inquiry, wherein Hatton, Lauderdale's brother, had embezzled the staggering sum of seventy two thousand pounds. In punishment, probably, with the realisation that such a sum could never be paid back, the King had the fine limited to twenty thousand pounds, which was to be shared out to deserving ministers of the Crown. In particular, the Chancellor, the Earl of Aberdeen stood to benefit most. Amidst the forfeiture were the lands and Castle of Dudhope. He who was lord of Dudhope was, by ancient right, the Constable of Dundee. For the Chancellor this had no appeal as he would have had to make it his residence, and besides, he was angling for the governorship of Stirling Castle. To John Graham this was, indeed, the `Inheritance of the Saints in Light`. It was sited only a mile away from his own lands of Claverhouse, it had the well appointed house, which he lacked, and it had the Constableship of the town of his birth. There was a sonorous ring to the words 'John Graham Constable of Dundee', pleasing, like the sound of a deep throated church bell, which had been rung down the ages.

At once Claverhouse expressed his interest, stating that if this dignity was offered he would be more than willing to purchase, from the Chancellor, the lands which lay about it.

Early in March, at the invitation of the Duke of York, Claverhouse went south to London, there to spend time in the enjoyment of horse racing, hunting, cock fighting and to have his brains picked by the Duke, as regards to things military and ways and means of keeping order in Scotland. The Duke was also keen that Claverhouse should become better known to his brother, the King.

Prior to his departure, learning that he was to go and to where, two pressing appointments were made with him. First, by Gordon, Earl of Aberdeen, who asked that his case for the acquisition of the Hatton fine be made, and, second, by, Queensberry who had his eye on the Dukedom, now vacant, since the demise of Lauderdale. Both asked that he press their cases for them.

From the outset Graham was amazed by the magnificence of the King's Palace of Westminster; the scale of it, its history, its gardens with their many sundials, the picture gallery made instant appeal. As you entered by the Cockpit Gate House, the creation of Holbein, the eye was at once struck by the way all of the parts went to make up a unified whole; the sweep of the Tilt-yard, where mail clad knights had jousted, the gardens beyond and the suites of buildings, and, delight of delights, the tennis court, where King Hendry the Eigth had played many a game. Perhaps Claverhouse might manage to play the Duke of York on it?

"I note that you spend much time in viewing the pictures of the gallery", said King Charles".

"Indeed, your Majesty I do. Please forgive me for not hearing your approach. I had become so engrossed as to be oblivious to anything but the art".

" Have you seen the Saint George, by Raphael? It is amongst my favourites. King Hendry the Eigth had it commissioned. It has a majestic quality, which once you have looked on it you are never likely to forget".

In the next forty minutes, spent with the King, Claverhouse was deeply impressed by his knowledge of art and his love of the paintings. With enthusiasm the King explained how the collection had been started by Henry the Eighth, and how his acquisitions had become the nucleus of King Charles the First's collection.

"Indeed", said the King, " I am a mere child, compared to my father, for it was his acumen and perception which caused the collection to grow, and, his knowledge of art, which was as profound as that of any other expert, which led to the acquisition of most of the great works you see, here."

"In particular, Sire, I must admit, I have a preference for the

Titians, they have spontaneity, without any hint of excess, you can feel that his brush was his instrument of expression. Also, his use of deep and intense colours is superb; never have I seen such vibrant use of reds. It has been my privilege to view these master pieces, for which I thank you.".

"You must not underrate the others, in particular the works of Holbein and those of Raphael. My father showed me how Holbein's works were truly models of objectivity. His style was unique and he had the ability to present an uncannily shrewd insight into human nature. Raphael's colours were clarified and he could heighten loveliness and grace. His landscapes have great purity, with luminous atmospheres, and, in his religious themes, he presents a splendour purged of all fear and cleansed of the evil of Satan. At any time, feel free to view them. It is heartening, to me, that you have this enjoyment and appreciation. My brother, though he has spoken often of your martial efforts and loyalty, he has never told me of your love of art. I must bid you adieu, for other matters press, but we will meet again here, and perhaps, we can both learn from each other. I would be pleased if you would study the portrait of Nelly Gwynn, which I had done by Sir Peter Lely, and then you can give me your comments on it at a later date. She seems more than pleased with it. Nevertheless, I feel he has not caught the captivating quality of her eyes".

In a heart beat Charles was gone. Only the whisper of his slippers, as he padded off, hung in the air. Far off bells rang. Maybe, almost beyond the range of hearing, sibilantly, the River Thames also whispered, as it went down to the sea.

There was little time to weary or think of home for Claverhouse, caught up in the whirl of the Court. He did not care much for cock fighting, which the King was addicted to, though as a matter of courtesy he had to attend when invited; hunting in Windsor Park with the Duke of York, or horse riding in St.James Park had a much greater appeal. There were meetings to be attended, with the Duke, at St.James Palace, wherein matters of policy, in Scotland, were gone into in detail. Often, however, the talk would turn to things military, of Claverhouses experiences and of the Duke's. There was no doubt about Jame's bravery in battle, or the fact that he had the ability to reflect, in depth on tactics used or on those which might have been employed to better purpose. He had served under Henri, Vicomte de Turenne, for whom he had the highest regard. However, this was tinged with regret, for James had been forced, for political and economic reasons to fight for Spain, at his brother's, insistence, under Don Juan-Jose, suffering a crushing defeat by Turrene, near Dunkirk. There were tales, too, of the sea when James, as Lord High Admiral, had fought the Dutch, with one famous victory, off Lowestof, where five thousand Dutchmen had been killed and twelve Capital ships sunk.

In the evenings, often, the King would play Baguette, some times with as many as twenty members of the Court engaged either in play or spectating, or conversing together, in small groups. At first Claverhouse was stunned by the fact that some evenings there could be upwards of two thousand pounds, in gold coin, on the table. Later he was to learn that, in the last three months, Lady Castelmaine had twice lost upwards of twenty thousand at a sitting.

One night Hortense Mancini, Duchess Mazarin, the most celebrated woman in Europe appeared. At once the whole ambience of the room was transformed, just by her presence. Her hair hung to her waist, in a fall of obsidian, he rich tumbling curls black velvet, like a river of night. Her dress was deep blue. At her neck a single rope of pearls. She looked around taking in everything in a single sweep.

To Claverhouse's discomfort she left her attendant ladies and made straight for where he sat. He rose to acknowledge her.

"So, you are the Clavers of whom I have heard so much, the Soldier from the North".

"Madam, I am honoured to meet you".

She laughed, a high musical sound.

"Soon I must go, however, if you should care, being a military man, I shoot, with pistols, three times a week, in the Tilt Yard, perhaps you may like to join me, or, twice a week, I fence, at Monsieur Duclos's Accademy, where you are welcome to challenge me to a bout?".

"Perhaps the pistols might be best, for we cavalry men are used to the heavy sabre, not the rapier of the fence. You must be made aware that it is over two years since last I fired a gun. However, it will be my pleasure to meet you in the Tilt Yard".

With no more ado she turned and walked away out of the room.

Behind her, hanging on the air, she left a delicious, haunting scent, to tantalise the nose; unique only to her. But it was her eyes, which most of all, Claverhouse would remember. It was said that as the light changed so did their colour. To him they had appeared to be the hazel brown of the soft neck feathers on a grouse's ruff, with tiny golden filaments, which shifted and moved, as tides would flow, pulsing with life. He promised himself that if he had the good fortune to meet her again he would look to the colour of her eyes.

It was a fine morning, with high cloud, bright sunshine and only the lightest of breezes off the river. Blackbirds were calling to each other, making music in the shrubs. Of a certain, conditions for shooting could not be more perfect. Already two trestles had been set up, with a plank between, along which were placed apples, equally spaced out, the targets to be shot at. Already a crowd had gathered to watch the match..

Hortense appeared. Claverhouse was thunder struck, for she came dressed in men's clothing. He had never before seen a lady do so. Later he was to learn that she did not recognise women's conventions as such. Perhaps her great beauty, her upbringing at the French Court, her uncle being Cardinal Mazarin, the second richest man in Europe, lent her the feeling that she could flaunt precepts, and, when she chose, could shock. One thing she could never do was to hide her beauty, for even in men's clothing there was no hiding her womanhood. Today her hair was drawn back tightly and held with golden combs, black basalt on new fallen snow. And, indeed, her eyes were different, palest topaz, lucent, the colour of peat stained water, on a falling spate, in a mountain stream.

A wooden case was opened to reveal a matched pair of wheel lock steel pistols, embedded in purple cloth.

" You may chose which ever weapon you so wish. Each is right handed and identical. We will shoot turn about, each with five shots, at fifteen paces, twenty paces, and at twenty five paces. Perhaps, you would like to have some trial shots to get the weight and feel of the gun?"

"No Madam, that will not be required. Please proceed".

As Hortense took her stance behind the sawdust line on the

ground and prepared to fire Claverhouse examined his gun. It was a thing of beauty, with hunting scenes let into the metal, picked out in fragments of either bone or elephant tooth. It was much lighter than a horse pistol, being only nine inches long as opposed to those of fourteen inches, to which he was accustomed. The butt was also much less curved, having only a very small angle from the line of the barrel. It felt strange in his hand.

With a sharp, clear report the Countess shot, an apple soared into the air. She laughed with delight.

Carefully, Claverhouse took aim and fired. His chosen target did not move. Ruefully, he shook his head.

"It will take time for you to become used to my toy", Hortense said. Again she aimed and fired. Another apple flew.

Claverhouse shot once more, missing as before.

With four more shots his opponent removed the fifth apple. In turn Claverhouse had one hit.

In the sequence at twenty paces Hostense again hit five apples, Claverhouse three.

"See, I told you that you would need time to come to know the pistol".

At twenty five paces Hortense downed four apples. Claverhouse's tally was two.

"Sir, do not be downhearted, for of the last six people I have competed with, only one has bettered your score, and he had the advantage of having used these pistols twice before".

'Thank goodness I did not venture to suggest the swords', thought Claverhouse. 'She is indeed une-dame formidable'.

A fine pattern of lines touched the corners of her mouth as she smiled. Her eyes, Claverhouse noted, were once more different, having become the palest, luminescent yellow, the wondrous colour of comb honey, newly taken from the hive; alert, seeing all, but giving away nothing.

For all of the rest of his life Claverhouse knew that he would always remember her eyes.

X. THE BOOK.

There was much to read in the journal, reports of court cases, details of legal judgements, political considerations, hand drawn maps, some by himself and many which had been given to him; there were also passages set down, of his personal thoughts, and also, the thoughts or opinions of others. Over the years it had filled. Soon it would be time to start a second volume. Under his hands he felt the texture of the leather cover, now grown soft and smooth with continuous use. Knowledge was power. To know of a person's likes or dislikes, or their bent on a specific subject, often permitted an argument to be won or an advantage to be gained. All of his life he had listened to and learnt from his father ---- what better teacher than the pre-eminent lawyer in all of the land?

The book had come to mean much. It gave him great pleasure to trawl through it, particularly, in the evenings, to come upon something written long before, which could be read and savoured, or, which might require amendment in the light of the passage of time, or of new knowledge. Or there might be additional events to record and take note of, to store in the mind.

Over the years he had been assiduous in building up a network of contacts, from every walk of life, who fed him information on all manner of subjects, which were analysed, sifted, and, anything considered to be pertinent, or likely to be of use in the future, was written down.

Frequently, he sat long into the night, drinking claret, whilst he read, savouring the written word as well as the rich red wine. On occasions, well into the second bottle, sleep would overtake him and he would doze off in his chair; then the dream would come. It seldom varied. He saw himself in a world where every man would be at peace with his neighbour, and that peace would have come, because, he, John Dalrymple, had the belief and knew, because of his devotion to the betterment of mankind, that he was the chosen, the instrument, to bring about the engineering of it. It was shown to him that it would require struggle and an iron will to achieve the object and to overcome the many obstacles and difficulties which would be placed in the way of reaching it. What a goal to strive towards. What a goal to win. The ghosts of history danced inspiringly. Surely, he, who could contrive such an end, would perpetuate his name for all time? Greatness hung, like the evening star, beckoning, almost within his grasp. All that was needed was for him to reach out and take it.

In the morning, when he awoke, after the dream, he felt at ease, and his was the certainty, that in working for such an end, he would gain inner peace. Little did he know that he was drunk and reckless, fuelled by the toxins of craved for power. Ambition ran wild in his heart.

He had the conviction in his waking hours, that if peace could be achieved, then would come the golden years of prosperity for Scotland, perhaps, there might even be union with England? Into his mind came the remembrance of a passage he had read in the Bible, years before, in the Book of Ezekiel, which, at the time he had carefully noted in his journal, "I will make them one nation in the land on the mountains of Israel. There will be one king over all of them, and they will never again be two nations or be divided into two kingdoms". There was a sonorous sound to it, like the clash of cymbals or a fanfare of trumpets. It had total appeal to all of the Presbyterian principles his mother had drilled into him from his earliest years.

He brought his mind under control. It was akin to passing through a secret doorway into the place of power. In a moment he was aware of his destiny, with an intensity and clarity which almost overbore him. Power was a narcotic in his blood, stronger than poppy juice or the finest bottle of claret.

XI. NEWMARKET.

Audley End pleased Claverhouse greatly. In particular he was glad to be away from the hustle and bustle of London and the Palace of Westminster, though, now and then his thoughts turned to a woman with a black trail of hair and eyes of ever changing colour. Perhaps there would be time for leisurely rides out into the countryside of Cambridge or to visit the town itself, which the Duke of York had commended, often, for its superb architecture. Soon, he was to learn, that, that, was not to be. For, in ways, he was busier than he had ever been in London. In particular the King was addicted to taking long walks, and on finding out that Claverhouse was one of the few present who could match him stride for stride, he insisted on a long trek almost every day. Often these were of nine to ten miles duration. In this time Claverhouse began to have a clearer understanding of the King's Character, which was to prove to be more complex than he had anticipated. His breadth of knowledge on a wide range of subjects, from the arts, to history, to politics, to military strategy, to agriculture, to anatomy, to languages was astonishing, yet there was an underlying uncertainty, a lack of self belief which, even if it did not surface, too often, it was always there. Perhaps, that was why he needed strong willed women around him, why he was open to persuasion by flatterers, who often were insincere.

Cambridge, with its truly beautiful buildings, its gently flowing river, bordered by weeping willows, just coming into leaf; the many bridges, all united with timelessness to give an ambience of tranquillity and learning. Here the King's historical knowledge of the town was enlightening. He could reel off the names of each of the founders of the many colleges and the dates of their foundation. King's College Chapel, three hundred feet long, with its soaring fan vaulted roof, filled Claverhouse with awe. Charles was at pains to show him the newly installed Coat of Arms, in Wren's Library, at Trinity College, exquisitely carved from lime wood, by the master, Grinling Gibbons. Everywhere one chose to look, in this town, brought new wonders to the eye.

At Saffron Walden, near to Audley End, where they were in residence, the great regret was that the fields of crocuses were not in bloom, for the Duke of York had told Claverhouse of how, in the sun they blazed like molten gold. 'Where in all the world would you find enough cloth to use the dye from them?' It was little wonder that the Clansmen had saffron, as the favourite colour, for their shirts.

This was the first time that Claverhouse had had the opportunity of meeting the celebrated Nell Gwynn, though he had been well primed as to her, by the Duke of York. She proved to be pleasant, with a keen wit, given to practical jokes and to have a vocabulary, which, when she chose to use it, would have left many of Claverhouse's crudest troopers tongue- tied. There could, however, be little doubt of the affection she had for the King.

Newmarket was Claverhouse's greatest pleasure, for here he was amongst horses, which he loved dearly, and amongst men, whom, perhaps in any place, in all of Europe, knew more about the equine world, in all of its aspects. The Heath, vast and unspoiled, lay like a sea, split by the Devil's Dyke. Where could you find a piece of land more suited to the riding and racing of horses, or the coursing of hares?

"May I introduce you to Tregonwell Frampton?, the King asked of Claverhouse.

"My pleasure, Sire".

Previously, the Duke of York had informed him as to what to expect, and, in particular, had warned Claverhouse that Charles held Frampton in the highest esteem for his depth of knowledge of horseflesh, and, further, that he did not like to hear criticism of the man.

Foreknowledge was indeed, in this instance, very worth while, for Claverhouse had never before seen such an eccentrically dressed person, who obviously paid no heed, whatsoever, to the dictates of fashion. He wore a hat, of red and white checked material, pulled down on either side of his head, his jacket, unbuttoned, was of sepia brown, with tiny yellow hounds tooth specks, beneath this he sported an emerald green waistcoat, his legs were encased in what had once been a pair of loose fitting white nankeen britches, which were secured, in tucks, below the knees, with lengths of twine. On his feet he wore boots, which once might have been brown, but since they had never been polished and were much scuffed, was open to question. This, the man who loved horses, greyhounds, hawks, game-cocks and hated women before all else. At once Claverhouse took a dislike to him.

"We have come to see your mare, Bowstring, perform", said The Duke of York. "I believe you are to run her, in a fortnight's time, against the King's stallion, Rowley, for a purse of a hundred guineas?"

"Indeed yes", replied Frampton.

"May we see her run?" asked the Duke. "My friend James, here, will give her some competition over, say, two miles on one of the King's mares?"

When all was readied the two horses were off at the gallop. Very gradually, Claverhouse drew ahead, so that, on reaching the finish line, he led by about ten lengths.

"Well done, I don't think my brother has much to worry about when he runs Rowley".

Claverhouse was not so sure.' Had the horse been held up? He wondered? Had not Frampton run his horse Nutmeg against Lord Montague of Cowdray's unbeaten mare Lusty and won heavily, pocketing the huge sum of a thousand guineas?' Surreptitiously, on dismounting, Claverhouse, unobserved, ran his hand down over Bowstring's left fore fetlock.

That night, when sleep would not come, Claverhouse considered the problem, but could come to no conclusion, except his instinct told him that he was right to give the outcome further thought.

Days were a whirl of activity. When racing was in progress, the King would stance himself, along with his brother and Claverhouse, all mounted, at about five furlongs from the finish, then, as the competitors passed, they would take of at a mad gallop, urging the jockeys on, racing with them to the winning post, where congratulation or commiseration could be given, as was appropriate. Flying merlins at skylarks or gosshawks at hare or rabbit took up other days. It was near to impossible for Claverhouse to speak to the Duke at length, and it was borne in upon him that time was passing and he had not yet discussed the Subject of Dudhope, the Hatton Fine, or Queensberry's Dukedom.

The day dawned, at last, when the King and his brother had to be off about some business. Quickly Claverhouse rode into Cambridge on his own, arriving about noon. Enquiries had informed him that many of the horse racing fraternity frequented the Falcon Inn, so, to there he made his way. All was hustle and bustle , in fact he had difficulty in finding a seat, but eventually, on two people leaving he was able to squeeze in. Carefully scanning the crowd he eventually saw his intended target, one of the grooms who had been present when the mare Bowstring had run. He seemed very merry and Claverhouse decided that he had had more than a few drinks. On asking he was informed that the man was called Tom Thurlow. On attracting a barmaid's attention he ordered a jug of ale, which, when it was delivered, he had her set before the groom.

Rising from his place Claverhouse made his way to where Tom was seated.

"Well met, Tom, you will remember that last week I tried Old Rowley against Bowstring. Would you care to join me in a jar?"

With alacrity Tom was up, if a trifle unsteadily, and was seated at Claverhouse's table. They talked on horses in general. All the while Claverhouse made sure that his guest's tankard was kept full. Gradually Tom's tongue was loosened under the influence of the alcohol and by carefully steered conversation, which led him on to where Claverhouse desired.

"What do you think of Frampton's mare?"

"She is indeed a fine horse, as fast a one as you'll see on the Heath. She needs the right groom up to get the best out of her, but, on her day, few will beat her up to three miles, but a longer distance will find her lacking bottom, and a good stayer might give her a run for her money".

.Ale continued to flow and Tom's words began to slur.

"When does she exercise?" Tom, now supported on one arm and

leaning far over the table, with his other arm reached out and drew Claverhouse's head closer, in a conspiratorial manner. He tapped the side of his nose with a finger.

"If a man was to be up, early of a morning, very early, at least two hours before sunup, he'd see her run atween rows of torches, in the pitch dark. Black sometimes it is, black as the Earl o'Hell's waiscoat, an' cold too. You see, Frampton, he's a cool one, cards held close to his chest. Least seen, soonest mended, that's his motto. What the eye doesn't see the heart doesn't grieve about, that's Tregonwell's policy. He knows horses that one, but if nature can be helped along a bit, say for a guinea or two, Frampton 'll give it his best shot. Money is money an' if there is enough of it he can bend the rules in ways, to suit, that you'll never have heard of before or never even thought about".

With no more ado the drunk slumped forward, across the table, and was instantly asleep.

That evening, when the Duke of York had returned from a cock-fight, Claverhouse drew him aside.

"It will not be a fair race between The King's horse and Frampton's mare, when they race".

Quizzically the Duke's eyebrows rose." What makes you think so?"

"Because Rowley will run against Bowstring, which is not the horse I rode against".

Again the eyebrows rose. This time in disbelief."Bowstring is chestnut with white socks on both forelegs. She ran with all of her legs moving in parallel. The horse I raced in the trial throws her left foreleg out and when pushed runs crabwise. Besides, when I had the chance I ran my hand over the forelegs and it came away white, with, I suspect, a concoction of lime and size, which had been painted on. We must tell the King at once".

Silence hung. Then the Duke went into a shaking palsy of mirth. For nearly two minutes he laughed uncontrollably. At last, when he had calmed, though the corners of his mouth still crinkled, he was able to speak.

"This the best thing I have heard, in months, the bravado of Frampton, the cheek of the man; it is wonderful. I forbid you to give

Charles or anyone else the slightest hint of it. We will look forward to the outcome".

"I -----------". Claverhouse, thinking better of what he was about to say, let it trail into nothingness. 'Perhaps it would be a great jape?' Sincerely, he hoped, oh so sincerely, that it would not backfire.

There was a hint of spring in the air, perhaps the first warmth of the year, though it was still prudent to wear clothing that gave some protection. A breeze came, fitfully, from the south-west. Above, great clouds marched in procession, imperiously white against the blue of the sky. Birdsong was all about, skylarks poured forth their souls, warbling as they rose in vertical flight, rising ever upwards until they were lost from sight. Already a considerable crowd had gathered, all anxious to see Old Rowley run against Bowstring. Frampton was there, presiding over the preparation of his horse. As usual his total disregard of how he dressed was apparent. He wore a coat, at least three sizes too large for him, the hem almost sweeping the ground. On his head was a shapeless cap graced, incongruously, with a single peacock's tail feather.

Nell Gwynn came in her carriage, drawn by two matched greys. She had a love of horses, but, since she had had a bad fall, she had never again ridden. As always she was gay, acknowledging any acquaintance. Her hair, touched by the sunlight blazed redish brown, in gloss and hue, matching the chestnut of Bowstring,s coat. Seeing that the King was engrossed in talk with his groom she alighted from her carriage and made her way over to where The Duke of York and Claverhouse stood. Her face came alive, filled with light. The wind had brought carnations pinking to her cheeks; she seemed to carry sunlight with her.

"Goodmorrow, how think you that Old Rowley will run?"

Quizzically the two men looked at each other.

"Nell", said the Duke," I have it from the horses mouth that Bowstring will win the day".

"Surley not? Charles tells me that Rowley is in fine fettle".

"If I were you", replied the Duke," if you intend to place a wager, in his favour, I would make it a small one, nothing outrageous".

Her blue eyes lit up. "Perhaps I am wrongly informed, or perhaps you know more than you are prepared to say?"

Full of meaning the question hung dancing on the air, the Duke choosing not to answer it. For his part Claverhouse hoped he would not be asked. But, already Nell had espied Frampton and her penchant for playing practical jokes had taken over; knowing of his extreme detestation of women, she approached him.

"Ah, Mister Frampton, a good morning to you. May I compliment you on your dress sense. The coat you are wearing is of quite the finest cut I have ever seen. Keep up the good work. I have no doubt that you are the talk of Cambridgeshire. When I return to London I will tell all and sundry of how, you sir, are years ahead of anyone at Court or dare I say even in Paris, which claims to lead the way".

Before Frampton could reply she spun on her heel, mounted up into her carriage and was off for the race finish line.

Quickly the King, the Duke his brother, Claverhouse, and a posse of riders mounted up and were off for the winning post, leaving Lord Montague of Cowdray in charge of starting and to act as race referee, in case of dispute.

After a sufficient time had elapsed for the spectators to settle Lord Cowdray called the two horses forward to the sawdust start-line. Old Rowley, the huge black stallion was the calmer of the pair. He seemed to balance himself between the rider and the earth. From ears to tail his spine was supple and open, from whence his tailbone flowed out, curving down, in a graceful arabesque, whilst the breeze caressed the silken hairs of his tail into effortless motion. Bowstring, leery of the gathered crowd, crabbed sideways. She was at least two hands smaller than Rowley, but well proportioned, with a strong back and legs.

With a downward seep of his arm Lord Cowdray dropped his white handkerchief and the two contestants were off. By the three furlong post Bowstring was already six lengths clear, running with an easy floating motion, neck out and tail flowing straight behind.

Already the groom on the King's horse was considering using the whip, but was aware of the owner's displeasure at over application of the crop, he refrained from its use. By halfway the gap had opened to fifteen lengths and Rowley appeared to be struggling, spume gathering along the sides of his nose and forming on his neck in a creamy curd. Now, caution thrown to the wind, the groom was using his heels and applying the whip, willing the stallion to run faster. Imperceptibly Rowley began to cut the gap, nearing Frampton's horse as they galloped.

Now the waiting mounted spectators were in a frenzy, yelling at their favoured horse, urging it on, willing it to succeed. As Bowstring passed the four furlong to home post the horsemen took off riding like furies for the finish, halooing and voicing encouragement, in a clamour of sound.

In a last final effort Old Rowley picked up the pace, his stride lengthening, reaching out, driving for the winning post, great divots of earth flying back from his hooves. Mercilessly the whip went on, the groom now up along his neck It was, indeed a great try, but all too late, the chestnut winning by some six lengths.

At once the King reached for his purse, which contained the hundred guineas, tossing it to Frampton, who caught it effortlessly, skilfully plucking it from the air.

"It was a fine run, your Majesty. If it had gone a further mile I have no doubt your horse would have won".

With aplomb Charles hid his disappointment. A smile broke out on his long face. "Tregonwell, you rogue it was indeed well done. Perhaps you will join me later to enjoy a drink in the Falcon?"

Next day Claverhouse, at last, had his chance to speak with the Duke of York. The King being off somewhere with Nell.

"James, I would value your advice on three matters, which if I can prevail upon you, you may wish to take up with the King. You, yourself can perhaps decide on the first two, but the third will be the prerogative of his Majesty. **First**, there is the subject of the Hatton fine, which the King has already said should be allotted to persons involved in the governance of Scotland. May I suggest that The Chancellor, in view of his loyalty and commitment, is the person most deserving of any award? **Second**, as you know, the estate of Dudhope is involved, and, having a long and personal involvement with the town of Dundee, I, for myself, would make a plea for the title to it. **Third**, perhaps the most delicate of all, Queensberry has his eye on the Dukedom, now vacant, which was Lauderdale's. Many, in Scotland, now consider that it would help to redress the balance of the whig Dukedoms held by Hamilton and Buccleuch. Obviously the King will have very definite views on the subject, as to suitability and the political impact. Nevertheless, in confidence, I was asked to bring it to your attention."

"It is not often you speak for so long and I know you for your directness. These are indeed weighty problems to consider. Let us have a glass of Madeira, whilst I ponder on what you have said".

The wine poured each man began to drink. As the Duke lifted his glass the dark red liquid caught and refracted the light. With studied deliberation and total enjoyment, with not a further word, happy in each others company they proceeded to quaff the carafe.

"By the way, Court business presses, and we must return to Windsor in two days time".

At last word came that Claverhouse was to attend the Duke of York in his private room in St.James Palace.'Surely this would be to hear the answers to the points he had raised on his own behalf and for the Chancellor and Queensberry?' Being desirous of some support, particularly in respcct to Queensberry's title, Claverhouse had asked Melfort, the Joint Secretary of State for Scotland to accompany him.

Business like, the Duke sat behind a huge desk, which was covered with papers and writing equipment. At once he greeted Claverhouse and Melfort.

"Secretary, it is indeed a pleasure to see you. I trust your sail on the packet from Leith was smooth?"

"How goes the day with you John, I trust you do not tire of Windsor?"

"How could one in such a marvellous place? Is it your intention to attend the King's Easter Ball, there?"

"I would not miss it for the world. Let us, however, talk on more mundane things. All of the matters you raised I have put to the King, who discussed them with me at great length. As to the Hatton fine, The Chancellor is to be allotted sixteen thousand pounds of it, the other four thousand the King has ruled you will have it".

Claverhouse was stunned, never had he ever thought of any of it coming to himself. It was a princely sum indeed.

"With regard to Dudhope it shall be yours".

A charge of raw excitement ran through him.

"James, you and the King are too kind. I thank you both from the bottom of my heart. You will please convey to him my sincere thanks".

"You were best to do so yourself, at the Ball. Even Kings are not above enjoying thanks" A small curl of amusement touched the Duke's lips. "Queensberry will have to wait, for the King feels that, recently, he has distributed too many titles, and for now he does not intend to award any others. That does not mean he bears any ill will towards Queensberry He considers that, perhaps, in a year or two, the time will be more propitious. Further to the talks between us, when you return to Scotland, we will have set up a Circuit Court, to which you will be the military escort. The purpose of this Court will be to put the laws vigorously into execution against all persons found guilty of fanatical disorder or allied irregularities. Remember this, John, sometime back, you said something profound, which the King and I have never forgotten and have treasured. Namely,' that you detested rebels because they violate the principles of authority and authenticity, which give your existence meaning, for without recognised authority you believe there can be no concept of the sacred'".

Melfort noted the rapport between the two men, but felt it best not to interject, for matters in which he had an interest seemed to be moving to conclusions he had foreseen or which were to his approval.

Business now being over they drank a brandy to the health "of his Majesty and to the future".

Everywhere was a blaze of light. Huge candelabra dangled from the ceiling of the Great Hall, and placed around the walls, at intervals, between the banks of seats, were single monstrous candles with their feet set in circular wreaths of flowers, at the Queen's instruction. In every known hue of colour the ladies moved, greeting friends, discussing the latest gossip, preparing for the dance, or dancing. Many of the men rivalled them, with styled perukes, lace collars, sleeves which flared at their wrists in a froth of fretted cloth and waistcoats which bore embroidered rosebuds, or running dogs, or intricate floral designs, as took their fancy. The buzz of conversation was loud, insistent, laughter hung in the air, ebbing and flowing. In the gallery the orchestra performed, doing their best to be heard.

A hush fell, the music ceased, the Master of Ceremonies rapped imperiously on the floor with the heel of his staff." My Lords, Ladies and Gentlemen, the King and Queen".

Charles came, soberly dressed, but in perfect taste, with the Queen upon his arm. She wore a dress of blue with tiny white bangs around the hem. At her throat she had a single rope of palest tourmaline. With elegance, unhurriedly, they paced around the chamber, stopping, now and then to greet someone they knew and then they took the floor to dance.

Never one for exuberant dressing Claverhouse wore grey with blue piping all down the front. At his chest, on its silver chain, he sported the treasured watch, which had been given to him by the Duke of York.

True to form, a practice she was noted for, the Countess de Mazarin came late. With aplomb she entered. At once every eye was on her, male and female. The men for her beauty, the women to see what she wore. Slowly, she turned her head to survey the company, as she did so the wing of her hair swung in the flickering of the candles, touched with myriad points of light, which coalesced, as sunlight would on a raven's wing, imperceptibly fading into total blackness. Her dress brought gasps, for none had seen the likes of it before. It had only one sleeve, her right arm was bare from the shoulder down. But, what a sleeve; on it, delineated in tiny seed pearls, was a snake, its eye a blood red ruby, the mouth agape, with its poised fangs formed of garnets. As her arm moved so did the serpent, as if it lived. At two hand spacings the skirt had, sewn to it, feathers of the ostrich, from which the quills had been withdrawn, to make them lighter than swansdown; so that, when she turned in a dance, the ends flared into a false skirt, which floated at the full and then slowly subsided to magical effect, elegant and hypnotic to all. The contrast of her night black hair and her skirt, twin to the snowy windblown arabesques of the maytime blossom of the hawthorn, held her face in a shadow of impenetrable grace.

Deep in conversation with Samuel Pepys, who had been, with the Duke of York, largely responsible for making the navy into the fighting force it had become, Claverhouse was startled when addressed.

"So, we meet again Colonel Graham. How was your trip to Newmarket? I trust that you did not loose too much money with the horses? Perhaps, if you are not otherwise engaged I may have the next dance with you, a Gavotte I believe? Please, you may now call me 'Ortense', for since the shooting we are good friends, no?"

"My dear lady, it is my pleasure, and though I do not shoot well, I must warn you I dance even more badly"

She smiled and her eyes were a wondrous colour, aureate, as early morning light- touched- dew on the petals of a suncup.

Quickly the floor was taken by the dancers, who dressed off in setts of eight. With a flourish the orchestra struck up, the crumhorns, lutes, cornets and sackbutts breaking into "The Dance of the Little Feet".

Turn and turn about the lead couple danced in the middle of the sett, and as each passage ended the males would kiss their partner's hand, then process to kiss the hands of the other three ladies.

In the dance Hortense moved with a tantalising, colt like elegance, which combined with the novelty of her robe, to make them the very centre of attraction for all assembled.

Aware of her beauty Claverhouse was gladdened by it. Each time he kissed her hand he knew an excitation, which he had never known before. Her eyes fathomless, so deep a man could drown in them. Soon, he must go north, but he knew that he would not forget her;--- wilful, independent, spirited, these were the adjectives that he would recall her by; the picture of her face indelibly etched in his mind ----and the eyes, ah, those eyes, ever filled with mischief.

XII. THE SWORD.

For some time MacIain had known that a crack had developed in the point of his sword, but due to the pressures of his Clan duties and the distance to Dalmally he had held off having it repaired. Now, he would have to have it seen to as the point had snapped off.

"It's a bonny weapon", said MacNab, the smith." Old too, and finely crafted".

"It was my father's and his father's before that. So I treasure it and would not part with it ".

With the eye of an expert MacNab examined it closely, looking up every now and then to appraise MacIain. " Have you ever thought of having a new sword?" he asked.

"No, never, this of my ancestors will do me fine".

"Well, for a man of your size the sword is much too small."

"It's done me a turn or two", I would have need of a weapon till the new was ready".

"I have four swords in bye the house, you would be welcome to take which ever suited you, to use until yours was ready. As to how long it would take I would need three months clear, for this would be like no blade you've seen before".

That this was no idle boast, MacIain knew, for, for all of the sword smiths in the Highlands, MacNab was rated the best.

"Very well then, make it"

With infinite care MacNab took measurements from MacIain, using lengths of twine, from armpit to wrist, from wrist to the end of the fingers, to the ascertained dimensions.

"I've forged many swords in my time, but none have ever been the size that you need. MacIain you're a big man".

"Right then I'll be back in three months to see what you've crafted".

Water dripped off the ends of the dead heather stalks, which protruded from the slick black vertical face of the peat hagg. As the gathering light touched each drop it gleamed silver. With care Macnab looked all around, making sure that he was unobserved. By eye he lined up a notch in the hill to the west, moved five feet to the left, again lining up an old stone cairn to the south. When he was satisfied, that he was in the right place, he began to dig into the rich peat. In a short time metal struck on metal. Quickly he uncovered a bundle of iron rods, bound together with leather thongs. They were just as his father had left them eighteen years before. With a cloth he cleaned the peat off every rod, examined them and selected a dozen, which he considered to be the best. Then, taking each in turn he ran his tongue up each side of each rod, feeling for those with the least impurities. Satisfied, at last, he chose eight. Carefully he rebundled the rods he did not want and buried them once more in the peat. Soon he would need to bury eight rods, of similar quality, to make up the number, and, soon he would need to show his eldest son where they were hidden.

Whaups called from high up on the hill, their burbling calls sounding out over the landscape. To the north a heron flew, seemingly slowly, its flight deceptive, legs a trail, the large wings moving with apparent indolence. In the birch trees titmice called incessantly one to the other, sharply and incisively.

All of the air was filled with the smell of burnt metal, charcoal and the sweat of the smith, pungent, acrid, overpowering. In the forge the fire glowed orange. With care MacNab had sorted out the charcoal, ensuring that he only picked that which had been made from alder. He used that of beech and ash, but, for the purpose of making this sword, he preferred alder; for, of all the charcoals, it was the best for holding an even level of heat and could be quickly brought up to temperature when air was blown through it.

It was important to use every possible piece of magic, in the creation of a supreme blade, even if it meant invoking the help of the fairies, together with every ounce of skill and knowledge acquired over the years. His father had told him that he would know when to dig up the peat cured bars, 'for it will only be given to you once, maybe twice and rarely, if ever, a third time to make a great sword. When it happens you will know'.

Nine was the spell-number to be used, so the smith took the eight bars and together with the old blade of MacIain's he started work. Instructing his son as to how he wanted the bellows pumped he had the bed of charcoal brought up to the temperature that his eye alone knew the sight of. When the mass of the bars had attained the heat necessary he withdrew them and began to hammer weld them on his anvil, taking care to work MacIain's blade into the other bars. Time upon time they were reheated, rehammered, reheated again, and rehammered. When the metal was drawn out to length, it held the fire-bloom and the blue mackerel stripes of the woven welds, which bound the nine strips into one broad blade. Already, the smith knew that it had begun to live. Each day of work made it grow, from the dense smalt shaft it had been, into a single broad blade. Later, he brought the edges out, tapering them from the central spine. Then, when, at last, this was done, he used a former, which he had especially made, to insert a blood-gutter on each side. With infinite care he made sure that each gutter was of equal spacing, in order to ensure that the balance of the weapon would not be impaired. The point was drawn out, so that it would pierce, but it would not be so thin as to be weak.

Then came the most necessary and perhaps the most essential of all tasks, the tempering of the edges. Into a mixture of liquid, the recipe of which only he, together with his sons, had knowledge of; oil of the basking shark, urine of the horse, sap of the birch tree and a goodly dose of brandy, the heated blade was plunged. Only when the eye of MacNab was satisfied that the edges were of the correct heat-colour, which differed from that of the central shaft, for, the edges were always made harder than the blade. Hissing and steaming the steel was laid on a bed of frost white Lochaline sand and covered over with the same, wherein it was allowed to lie cooling slowly, for seven days.

Satisfied it was as he wanted the smith started to furnish the sword. Sparks flew as he hammered cold iron into a flat plate, then he shaped it into a hemisphere, beating it over a cress to give it its form, after which he split it into a basketwork of interlaced tendrils, the head of each one which he formed into a thistle. On the haft of the hilt he bound deerskin, securing it with copper wire, and in the pommel he set a large cairngorm stone, which, when polished, pulsed and coruscated in the light of the forge, the crystalline quartz giving of a smoky yellow gem-fire. His younger son, who had a delicacy of touch, took thin sheets of silver, heated them just below melting point. and with a tiny hammer beat it on to the thistle heads, so that it adhered there, enriching the hand guard. Last of all MacNab treated the blade with vinegar and arsenic to etch and enhance the patterns, and finally he punched in a series of tiny marks, the significance of which, to him, was unfathomable. However, his father had been adamant that they were of prime importance. For, down the run of time, the meaning of them had been lost, but the MacNabs had passed the knowledge down from father to son. Long ago, a Viking Rune Master had composed the words, and they read 'MacNab fire forged this sword for him of the line of Somerled'. For a fortnight MacNab's sons sharpened and honed the blade with pumice, under their father's watchful eye, until the light twinkled like tiny stars along its cutting edge.

There was an air of expectation about MacIain as he swung down off his garron at Barr a Chaistealain, on the slope above the township of Dalmally. Sunshine dappled the land, with the hills to the north standing clear. Quickly he made his way to the forge where MacNab was hard at work. Not wishing to interrupt, the Chief waited, until the smith had finished.

"You'll have come for your sword? It is indeed ready for you, though it took longer in the making than I had bargained for".

With no more ado he lifted a bundle of cloth and unwrapped the weapon, which was sheathed in a leather scabbard.

"I had the saddler at Lyx make the sheath, for a metal one is of no use, as it would blunt the edges".

MacIain saw that it, also, was a thing of beauty, for the saddler had patterned it, down the face, with embossed sprays of heather, the emblem of the Clan Donald. Anxious to see the weapon the Chief drew it. The sword was heavy with slumbering power, the force of the magic of the runes flowed into him. He lunged, his weight on his front foot, the sword flickering out like a snake's tongue. He swung it in great figures of eight, the song it sung as the air passed over the cutting edge a sibilant hiss. Light flashed on silver, on mackerel steel and Cairngorm gem-quartz, wonders to the eye. At once Glencoe knew that this was a sword before any he had ever wielded. It was a living thing, not only because of its worth as a weapon, but because it carried his dream, the essence of true self. In it dwelt his courage, his honour, his pride. Also it held the innate qualities, tooled by the run of time, passed down from father to son, in the blade of his ancestors.

"It truly is marvellous. There is no sword like it in all the land. You, alone, could have fashioned it", said MacIain.

'Praise indeed ', thought the smith.

"Now the proof of it will be how it is used and how it performs".

"What is the cost?" asked the Chief.

"Six cows will cover it".

This was a considerable sum, but MacIain knew that what MacNab had manufactured was beyond price, for a good sword was of infinite worth, before the finest racing stallion, or a scad of the fleetest deerhounds, unmatched.

"You will have them next week".

With that he signed to his tail of retainers, swung up on to his horse and took them down the brae at a brisk trot. A week later Inveriggan delivered six of the best cows Glencoe posessed, each with a calf at foot, together with an anker of French brandy and a fine woolen scarf, woven in MacNab tartan, for the smith's wife.

It seemed an excessive payment, to Inveriggan, but he knew from long experience, that it did not pay to question his cousin's decision on matters such as this.

For his part MacIain considered that the higher the price the more the subject would be bruited about, and the more it was discussed, the more of a legend it would become. Of such stuff were the reputations of Chiefs made.

MacNab knew that this was the finest sword he had ever made and that never again would he make its equal.

Mac Iain knew that it was the best sword he had ever wielded.

Neither man knew that it was rune-spelled.

"Well, Iain, I am hearing that you have a new sword, may I have a sight of it?" Angus nan Oran, Angus of the Songs, enquired of his brother, the Chief.

"That you shall".

With pride MacIain brought it, handing it over.

Carefully, Angus examined it, hefting it and testing its edge with the ball of his thumb.

"Man, but it is a work of art, though a bit long, even for me, and I am only a hand and a half smaller than yourself. Swing it for me, let it sing"

So, Mac Iain did so, swinging it in great figures of eight. The air whistling over the blade with an assonance that pleased the ear, as when a piper playing a pibroch achieves perfect pitch

"It has a magic sound", said Angus, "like the wind in the wings of the yellow-nosed swans, when they flight in to alight on the waters of Loch Achtriotachan".

"Brother, only a poet could put it so, but you have just named the sword. It shall be called Swan's Wing"

At that Angus was enchanted

Later, when Mary was told of it, she took the red cloth padding, which had been fitted by MacNab, out of the hand-guard, and replaced it with a cloth of sulphur yellow, to honour the swans, and out of fondness for her brother-in-law, and not forgetting the Chief.

XIII. THE HOMECOMING.

Immediately, on returning, Claverhouse reported to the Chancellor **first**, on the allotment of the Hatton fine, **second**, on the King's disposition, to himself, of Dudhope, **third**, on the matter of Queensberry's Dukedom, and **fourth**, to present the King's letter of appointment of Colonel Jame's Graham of Claverhouse to the Privy Council. There was little time for anything with the Circuit Court spending a week in each of the towns of Stirling, Glasgow, Ayr, Dumfries, and Jedburgh. Everywhere the Test Act was used as a gauge of a person's loyalty or as a pardon to those who lay under the possibility of a charge of treason for complicity in the Bothwell Rebellion. At Dumfries, Claverhouse did manage to steal a few hours to meet with his brother, to allow himself to be updated as to conditions in the West, which were not as he would have wished, with conventicles taking place and various other acts of rebellion having occurred. He also craved the deeds for Dudhope, but Hatton and his lawyers were tardy in their dealings and the matter drifted on. Often he dreamed of the house, set above the town, surrounded by its oaks and mature plane trees. For all of his life he had known it, sited above the majestic sweep of the River Tay, surely, soon it would be his?

In April, at last he had it, the Crown Charter. The dream was his. He had the mansion, the title of Constable of Dundee and he was the Colonel of Horse. Now, he could take his place at any level of society. There had been many trips from the West back to Edinburgh to attend the meetings of the Privy Council, in excess of thirty in the space of seven months. The meetings, in the main, proved to be of great interest, but at times he was irked by vacillation and indecision, which gave rise to Dundee, when matters referred to his area of operation, using the name of the Duke of York, during his Grace's continuing absence in London. There were those on the Council who took umbrage at this and stored up festering resentments. It was just the sort of behaviour to make him the bitter enemy of those who considered themselves to be his peers.

However, there was a compensation in all of this. When he had gone to Edinburgh to attend the Council, he had often been accompanied by Lord Ross, for whom he had the utmost respect, both as a soldier and as a friend, for his lordship had taken him to meet the Lord Dundonald. There, in the Cannongate, he had made the acquaintance of the Earl's grand daughter, the Lady Jean. In company with Lord Ross they had entered the Earl's drawing room, which was furnished with oak settles and tapestries, though the air of the room was sober, as would befit a committed Presbytarian.

She turned to greet them. At once Claverhouse was struck by her looks. Her hair was curled in cornrows, which fell to her shoulders in a wash of gold. Dundonald introduced them.

"Perhaps, if it pleases you, Colonel, Jean will sing to us?"

At that instant Claverhouse could think of nothing better.

Ross played at the spinet, Lady Jean sang. Her voice was sweet, not full, but pleasant. Claverhouse was enchanted. There was that about her which he was never able, afterwards, to define, but, which indelibly etched itself upon his soul, whimsical, haunting.

As the evening progressed Claverhouse, despite Lord Dundonald and all of his family having the reputation of being "black fanatics", found himself liking the old man more and more; he proved to have tact and maturity. That he was well educated and had a wide knowledge on many subjects was soon apparent. On that of poetry, which was one of Claverhouse's favourites, he could recite several of Dryden's, and one or two of Milton's, some of Shakespear's sonnets, and surprise, surprise, he had a liking for Claverhouse's favourite, Lucan. He had also a great store of anecdotes on the history of Scotland and its associated antiquities.

Every now and then Claverhouse found himself stealing a glance at the Lady Jean.

All too soon it was time for John and Lord Ross to leave. They thanked their host and his granddaughter for their hospitality and said their farewells.

Often, when his duties permitted, Lord Ross, would visit his cousin, the Lady Jean and her widowed mother, at "The Place", at Paisley, and sometimes he brought his Commanding Officer. Each time Claverhouse found himself drawn more and more to Jean; each time he could not wait for the next occasion to come round. For the first time, Claverhouse knew that he was falling in love with the twenty year old, who was fourteen years his junior. That this could present so many obstacles and difficulties he had never foreseen or even thought about. Most troubling of all was Jean's mother. Presbyterianism had leached the soil from her soul and left it as a desert. Should a seed-corn , by accident ,fall upon it, it would lie forever sterile, for there would be no spark to quicken it to life. In the Heaven she craved to reach would the Maker smile when she entered? Her eyes were edged with mistrust, unreadable, the windows of her mind closed to all but God and the promise of salvation, veiled from earthly things, cloaked in evangelical virtue. She and Jean were often in conflict over the very simplest of things. Indeed, Claverhouse came to realise, and to admire, that Jean was her own woman, whether in the holding of opinions which differed from those of her parent, or of anyone else, for that matter. There could be no doubt that the mother, the Lady Catherine, was of the mind that Claverhouse was unsuitable for her daughter in every way; she, in fact, though not in his presence, referred to him as "The Persecutor".

Obstacles, hindrances, and problems came from quarters which Claverhouse had never even considered, being of the belief that the taking of a wife was the concern of no one but himself. In particular The Duke of Hamilton and Queensberry caused him much grief. For Hamilton's part he considered that everyone gave too much attention to Claverhouse and not enough to himself. He poured out his venom to Queensberry, who, unexpectedly, lapped it up. Queensberry, in turn, was of the belief that Claverhouse had not pressed his case for the Dukedom, with sufficient vigour, in London, with the King and the Duke of York. This pair colluded in attempting to point out Claverhouse's disloyalty. Queensberry penned a letter to the Duke of York on the subject, but was roundly rebuffed by the reply, which treated him with some contempt and let him know that James, and his brother, the King," in all the Land, could find none more loyal than John Graham". As a footnote Queensberry was asked "not to be a damned fool".

Edinburgh society, ever agog for scandal, was ready to snigger at "the champion of conformity being led, by the nose, by a daughter of the enemy". Besides, all of Jean's relations were suspect in the eyes of the Government, being looked on as "Presbyterian fanatics". Jean was obviously religiously unsuitable.

In order to compound the charge of disloyalty Hamilton, whose daughter was being courted by Lord Ross, made great play of not giving her hand until he had the permission of the Duke of York and the King. This eventually forced Claverhouse, who had not previously considered it to be necessary, to ask for royal approval.

XIV. The Wedding.

No one could have wished for a better day, the sky was almost cloudless. A soft breeze blew out of the west. To the east the River Cart ran summer low, hesitant to give its waters to the Clyde, slow in the main, but here and there moving in a sudden rush, chuckling in its bed. Starlings, handsome in their wine coloured ruffs of feathers, chattered and chuckled, as in family parties they ran about, digging their beaks into the turf, probing for wire worms and the grubs of flies. Yesterday they had signed the Wedding Contract, but Jean's mother, unbending as ever, had refused. Indeed, she had stated, categorically, that "there was no way she would attend at the marriage". That was a blow to Jean, but over the years she had learnt to accept that her mother was always capable of adopting rigid attitudes, impervious to any argument.

With obvious pride Lord Dundonald brought his grand-daughter in on his arm. About her brow was a garland of wild bluebells. Her hair, in perfect cornrows, sculpted the shape of her head and fell to her shoulders in a wash of gold. In her hand she bore a posey of hyacinths, her favourite flower. Claverhouse was enchanted. Placed all about were vases of the same flower, giving off a delicate fragrance, which held the lingering memory of honey of the bumble bee; the purple blue deepening, where there was shadow, to a perfect velvet, where outline went and all became profound, deepest black.

Fire and the collapse of the tower had left the Abbey in a partially ruined state, but the western section continued to be used. Despite this, the eleven centuries which had passed since it had been founded, as a Priory, by St. Mirren had imbued it with the patina of age, which melded with its history to heighten the sense of reverence all felt within its shadow. Six High Stewards of Scotland were buried here, and from them had sprung the Stewart Kings.

The virulence of the times had intruded, indeed, even into this special day. Early in the morning a galloper had come with a despatch for Lord Ross, from the Commanding Officer General Dalyell. Even now, as he stood there, in the kirk, Claverhouse asked himself if, indeed, the General had meant the contents for Lord Ross, or if the intention had been to cause personal grief; for, as he knew, the General was none too friendly towards himself, and Dalyell would surely have known that Ross would appraise Dundee of the contents of the dispatch? At once, even as the ceremony progressed, preparations were in hand for troops to be readied for the off. In his mind's eye the image of the General flared, the bald head with the waist long beard and the penetrating gaze, but, in an instant it was swept away. Jean's presence transcended all. Their eyes met. She took his hand and from the touch everything flowed. Each felt the growing sense of wonder that they had found one in the other. Their hearts burned with a fierce joy.

Now, the ceremony over, they processed from the church, down the steps, at the main doorway, where, to the surprised delight of the newly weds, Dundee's officers, resplendent in their scarlet tunics with primrose yellow facings, formed a Guard of Honour. Whilst, tricked out in grey, the kettle-drummers beat a boisterous paradiddle and his trumpeters blew a fanfare. No doubt Ross had set it up.

There was one huge regret, his brother had not been able to attend, laid low with influenza.

Pleasantries had to go by the board. Time was of the essence. More than a hundred rebels had been sighted in the Blackloch area. With little ado Dundee went to the house of the Place and in fifteen minutes was dressed in his field clothes. He kissed Jean full on the mouth, to the cheers of his men. The scent of hyacinths lingered all about her. Easily he swung up into the saddle. Horses pranced, and amidst a gallant clatter of hooves the cavalcade moved off..

Jean did not weep. She had married a soldier.

For three days and nights they hunted diligently, quartering the ground, with little rest, but they did not come upon a single person they could apprehend.

No rain had fallen for six weeks so that they enjoyed conditions which made riding, over the bogs and moors, much easier than usual. All were disgruntled by the fruitlessness of the search, which, coupled with the lack of sleep led to the men and horses becoming increasingly fatigued. Reluctantly, Dundee had the troops stood down and ordered them to Dalmellington, to rest.

In three days Claverhouse was back with Jean. Their time together was short lived. Strife, again, in the South West called him back, but eventually he did manage to take his bride north to Dundee, where they were able to steal a fortnight together, before duty once more tore them apart.

XV. THE KILLING TIME.

It was a time of political change, with those in power and those on the fringes of power setting to each other as partners would in a Highland Reel or the "Drops of Brandy" dance. Favours for services previously given were called in, or promises of future patronage were made, if support was offered. Past enemies were courted. Shifts in allegiance, to and fro', went on day by day. Innuendoes were bruited about, aspersions cast, footholds were scrambled for on ladders, whilst rungs on the same ladders were sawn through. The thirst for advancement, or advantage, was unquenchable.

It was ordained, by the King, that Scotland should be run by a Cabinet, Queensberry took Lauderdale's place, Perth succeeded Aberdeen as Chancellor. Melfort became the Secretary of State.

Filled with self- importance the men who ran the Church were drunk with hatred. They considered themselves to be divinely appointed to give advice on all things, whether legal, military or political. Above all they were the witch-hunters supreme. Ministers of the Kirk were the sole interpreters of God's Will, and, as such, were untouchable; answerable to no man. They could rabble rouse, leading their congregations to an excitation far above the humdrum of their everyday lives, make them delirious with rage. Weekly, the kirk sermons lifted them to a plane far above anything they had ever experienced. Agitators, trained in Holland, were brought in

In the South West a new Messiah appeared, James Renwick, who had been ordained in Gronigen , a gifted orator, a true zealot. With his followers Renwick affixed a declaration to the market cross at Sanquhar, which disowned the King. It stated that he had broken the Covenants and therefore was not a King, and was worthy of death. All of the authority of Charles Stuart was disowned.

With no further ado, alarmed by rebellion on such a scale, the Privy Council approved an order that anyone refusing to disown the Renwick Resolution, under oath, whether they were in arms or not, should be immediately executed before two witnesses.

Two soldiers were slain, followed by the murder of a minister, who had favoured the Government. Then, just before Christmas about one hundred rebels invaded the town of Kirkcubright, killing the sentinel at the Tolbooth, and releasing all of the prisoners held there, removing any arms they could find, and then they marched out, arrogantly, to the beat of the town-drum, which they had commandeered.

Claverhouse, with his dragoons, pursued them from Bridge of Dee to Auchencloy Moor, where a skirmish took place, ending in five rebels being killed and three prisoners taken. Now, in his heart, Claverhouse knew that he could no longer boast that "Galloway was as peaceful as any part of the country this side of Tay"

Other problems intruded. Suddenly, relations between Claverhouse and Queensberry became openly hostile. At no time had Queensberry ever considered that Claverhouse had prosecuted, with sufficient zeal, at Court, the quest for his ennoblement. Indeed, it seemed that the work, in London, had been rather for the advancement of Graham.

Filled with jealousy and spite Queensberry appointed his brother, James Douglas, to be the Commander in Chief of the army, a man who had been a lawyer. Whilst, to compound matters, he had his son, Lord Drumlanrig, promoted to the Lieutenant Colonelcy of Claverhouse's regiment. Two months later, another son, Lord William Douglas, was given a troop under Claverhouse's command.

Incensed, Claverhouse expressed his views without reservation; his resentment, at commands being handed out to persons who were ill trained or unqualified for military life, finally boiling over. At once Queensberry wrote to the Duke of York on the subject.

In November Queensberry became His Grace the Duke of Queensberry.

At a meeting of the Privy Council in December a petition was presented by some of Colonel Douglas's soldiers, registering complaints that they had been dismissed the Regiment, and that pay due them had been used to buy items of kit for other of the troops.

At once Claverhouse was on his feet. "This is a nonsense ", he thundered. " Would you have no one join the army? Are you, the members of the Council, aware that Colonel Douglas has dismissed Dragoons of long service, some of over twenty years, because they were not all of the same height, to improve the appearance of the regiment? Are you aware that the Colonel issued orders as to the length to which men were allowed to grow their beards, the dimensions of the ribbons they were permitted to use to tie their hair, and the kind of kerchiefs they could wear? I say again, this is nonsense. Men should be trained up in the pride of their regiment, in their loyalty to the King. Fighting men should not be the subject of fripperies or be tricked out in geegaws"

" You, sirrah, stand here before the Council, speaking of nonsense. I say that what you say is the nonsense. That the Colonel has resolved to improve the standing of his regiment should be looked upon by all as commendable". So, the Duke of Queensberry responded, in stentorian tones.

At once Claverhouse replied. "Your Grace", said with lips acurl, and with total disdain, "Men of the army are worthy of consideration, at all times, whatever their rank, whether they be simple privates or commanders. When any man enlists he is deserving of the consideration that befits his giving of service and within the rules of his commitment he should be accorded all dignity possible".

Apoplectic now, the Duke, in high dudgeon responded. "Do you deign to challenge the rights of those commissioned to command in the King's name?"

The riposte was instant. "I do"

Uproar broke out, with both the supporters of the Duke and of Claverhouse clamouring to make their points.

Swiftly, and with composure and fine judgement the Chairman hammered with his gavel. " This sitting of the Council I hereby adjourn in order to permit all parties to consider the matters touched upon".

That evening both the Chancellor and Melfort wrote to the Duke of York, reporting the fracas, placing emphasis on what they considered to be disrespect, by Claverhouse, to the Duke of Queensberry.

In turn, York wrote Queensberry informing him that when next in Scotland Claverhouse would be told that his behaviour towards the Duke was unsatisfactory.

Other faults attributed to Claverhouse were noised abroad, in particular it was given out that, because of his Cochrane connection, he had shown favour to the Whigs in Ayrshire. This was seized upon by Queensberry as an excuse to withdraw Claverhouse from his command in the West. To rub salt into the wound Colonel Douglas was moved into Galloway with his troops. Meanwhile Queensberry asked Melfort to look into the fines, which had been collected, previously, by Claverhouse, in Galloway. He also intimated that he thought Claverhouse should now be asked to pay for the "gift", four years before, of the estate of Freuch, in Galloway.

A fortnight later Melfort reported that the Duke of York would deal with the matter of Freuch, but he had authorised that any monies owing to the King, by Claverhouse, should be called in.

All of this came as a thunderclap, because of the money involved, also Claverhouse was disconcerted that he had not been given the opportunity to plead his case.

On the first day of February King Charles the Second became ill, taking to his bed, where he died on the sixth. His rightful heir, James, Duke of York became King.

Immediately, Melfort was, once more, describing Claverhouse's conduct as impudent and churlish. The King, busy with the affairs of State, had little time to consider the matter, but he was now beginning to feel uneasy about the affair; considering Claverhouse's past loyalty.

March came in like a lion, a chill east wind moaned and soughed, halooing like a lost shade, sharp and cold, out of the east, blowing through the pends and wynds of Edinburgh. With some trepidation Claverhouse went to attend the Privy Council, in answer to its summons.

All of his adversaries were there, he knew that they outnumbered his allies.

Without preamble Queensberry was instantly on the attack.

"What say you Graham regarding the Galloway fines acquired by yourself whilst the region was under your jurisdiction? Can you inform the Council as to the amount of them?"

With a studied slowness Claverhouse rose to his feet. His eyes swept the company, seeing all, betraying little of his feelings. There was pride in his carriage, one could not doubt that this was a soldier.

"Your Grace, members of the Council. The Sheriff-Depute of Wigton has the matter in hand, he is computing the figures at this very moment. May I ask that the Council allot to him the necessary time?"

"At most we will allow six days", snapped Queensberry.

"With all due respect I would point out that six days, given the distances to be travelled, to carry the information, is as if you give none".

"Then you shall have none", rapped out the Duke.

Towards the end of March Queensberry went to London and returned with even greater powers, having been appointed to be Lord High Commissioner to the Scottish Parliament. He, at once, confirmed that his brother was to take over Claverhouse's place in Galloway. The very next day Graham was stripped of his place on the Privy Council, on the pretext that, due to his marriage into a family of fanatics, he was not a fit person to know the King's secrets.

Now, only a soldier, stripped of his justiciary powers, Claverhouse gave himself over to the suppression of any rebellion in the West.

All night long they had been out on patrol, following up information on a group of men who had been seen acting suspiciously, on the western flanks of the Lowther Hills. Late on they had come upon them, but they had split up and most had been lost in the darkness, except for two, whom they had pursued for miles, splashing through bogs and burns. Often the dragoons were given to the thought that darkness was the fugitives' friend, but, somehow, they managed to come up with them again, under the cloak of the night, in the wolf-grey light.

At length, aided by the pale and bony fingers, of another lifeless dawn, which were now feeling their way across the sky, the land appeared, taking on form, as the night drained, and shapes emerged. Further off, the two men, in flight, could be dimly seen.

At Priesthill, in the parish of Muirkirk they were finally apprehended, at the cottage of John Brown.

In order to interrogate them Claverhouse had seated himself on a low bench, and had them brought before him, one at a time.

First he questioned the younger, who stated that he was Brown's nephew. Quickly, the Colonel realised that the youth was retarded and by judicious questioning important points of information might be had.

With John Brown, known as "The Carter" Claverhouse knew he had indeed met up with a prize, for this man had, the year before, been mentioned on "The Most Wanted Men Proclamation" issued by the Privy Council. Also, to crown matters, he had, two months before, been named as one of those excluded from indemnity, being a known associate of Renwick.

"Here Colonel, you'd better come and see what we've found", shouted out his Sergeant.

"You two troopers guard these men close". Claverhouse rose from his seat and went to see what was causing the excitement.

"Here Sir, in this chamber, below the turf we've found gear fit for war". So, indeed, it was. A small cask of gunpowder, three swords, a bag containing twelve musket balls and a pair of pistols; the weapons all greased and in serviceable condition.

Once more Claverhouse commenced his questioning. On several occasions he was interrupted by Brown's wife, who ranted at him. Each time he waited for her to finish and twice instructed her on points of law.

"Would you like me to take her off?" asked the Sergeant.

"Indeed no, let the woman stay".

Three times, in the course of the interview, Claverhouse, after explaining that there was no reason for him to do so, asked Brown to take the Oath of Abjuration, disclaiming Renwick. Each time Brown refused and fell to prayer.

"You are condemned by the evidence against you, of the arms secreted, and, more particularly, by your refusal to take the oath. In which case, by the Law, you are sentenced to death".

The detestation he felt for rebels rose in Graham. They violated the principles of authority, which gave existence its meaning. Without recognition of authority there was no concept of the sacred. His was the total belief in constituted authority. The law applied, ---------a soldier did his duty.

None of his troopers or the Sergeant, by their attitude and body language, was keen to carry out the sentence. He had for long half expected this situation to arise when the time came for a summary execution to be called for. Now, he was alone with the agony of command. There was no doubt, in his mind, that he could order the death sentence to be applied. However, he had been taught, from the earliest years of his military career, that an officer should not ask anyone to do anything he, himself, was unwilling to so do.

"Give me your pistol Sergeant" He took it, hefting it in his hand, checking the priming, turning, he aimed it at Brown and fired.

The ball struck the prisoner's forehead exiting through the back of his skull, spraying blood and pink brain-matter. In that instant he was dead.

With a wild scream Brown's wife ran forwards to cradle the head of her slain husband, her apron reddening with the seepage. She began to curse Claverhouse, who let her harangue flow around him until she ceased.

With all the dignity he could muster he addressed her. "To men I can be answerable, and, as for God, I will take Him into mine own hand".

Greenshanks flew wheepling through the sky, their mournful cries trailing after them as they went away into the distance; the most forlorn of sounds.

Wind rose, blew and then died, rose again and sighed, a long, lonely sussuration, sweeping over the sedges and deer –grass, sobbing sadly.

XVI. The Reinstatment.

Rumours abounded, in London and in Edinburgh, that Argyll and Monmouth were to invade. Between them they would create a Presbyterian state, with Monmouth, as King in England, and Argyll would rule in Scotland.

By now the King was having doubts as to the treatment of Claverhouse. In view of his past unswerving loyalty it seemed that things might not be as they were reported. Besides, there was no other military commander with such a record of faithful service, and few with such a grasp of strategy. On that count alone it was imprudent not to have him in the field. Could there be an orchestrated conspiracy against John Graham? With a great deal of thought King James pondered long on the subject and came to the conclusion that there were those in high places who wished Claverhouse no good. Forthwith, he instructed Moray to inform the Privy Council, and Queensberry, in particular, that John Graham of Claverhouse was to be reinstated to the Council, by his royal order.

Now, being over seventy, Dalyell was replaced, as Commander in Chief, by the Earl of Dumbarton, whose immediate task was to co-ordinate the defence against Argyll's coming.

In the long days of May Archibald Argyll landed at Campbelltown. At once, Dumbarton and Claverhouse were promoted to Brigadier. Things did not go well for the Invader, he attracted insufficient followers, inspiring few with trust. Even his own clansmen were loth to rise for him, perhaps, as the son of the man who had fled the field at the Battle of Inverlochy, deserting his kin, or maybe Archibald's punitive imposition of inflated rents on his tenants led to a marked lack of enthusiasm. Swiftly, his efforts came to naught and he was taken prisoner near Paisley, being sent from there to the

Capital, where he met his end under the "Iron Maiden", the Scots guillotine.

Monmouth faired little better, being defeated at the Battle of Sedgemoor, a month later, to face death, at the sentence, handed down by the notorious Judge Jeffreys.

In July Claverhouse formally resumed his seat on the Privy Council. Following which he went north to Dudhope to spend time with his wife and to attend to a raft of business which had built up, both for his estates and for the town of Dundee.

When the first leaves began to fall he went to London, where, he was warmly received by King James.

Subsequent, upon his return to Scotland, it was very obvious that Queensberry was now out of favour. Indeed, Queensberry was ordered to pay back to Claverhouse the sum of five hundred and ninety six pounds, sterling, which had been extracted from him, against the Galloway fines. The Duke was much put out at this.

Four days before Christmas Claverhouse received the plenary honour of his military career, he was gazetted to be Colonel - in – Chief of his own regiment, which was henceforth to be known as "His Majesty's Own Regiment of Horse". He chose, for the uniform, red coats laced and faced with yellow. His kettle drummers and trumpeters were to have their own livery. For the Colour Sergeant he had a yellow flag made with a red saltire cross, in the upper triangullette he placed the rose of England and in the lower triangulette the lion rampant holding, in the dexter paw, a sword.

XVII. Castle Stalker.

To reward the Stewarts of Appin, who had, down the centuries, always stood loyally by the Stewart Kings, and to show his displeasure of the Clan Campbell, Charles ordered, that, after fifty six years, Castle Stalker was to be returned, by the Campbells, to the Stewarts. There was great rejoicing in Appin. To have it once again in their possession, the ancient symbol of their patrimony, was to show that they had come again into their own.

In order to celebrate it was decided that they would hold a great feast for their friends. Apart from all of the Stewart Chiefs, Lochiel , Glengarry, Keppoch, MacDougall and MacIain were invited.

As they came in over the brae the Glencoe men saw before them the most picturesque of all of the views in Argyll. Below them lay the great expanse of the mud of the Laich Loch, empty now, its waters having receded with the tide. Far off the hills of Morvern and of Mull stood in majesty, cloaked in every shade of blue, holding, in their hollows, crumpled shadows, their faces stark and ageless. But, at once Castle Stalker took the eye, a fastness of grey stone rearing in pride, roofed with huge slabs of Sleat slate, standing on its sea girt rock, with a yellow and blue banner flapping proudly above it, in the wind.

On the mud multitudes of waders were busy, whimbrel and curlews, plovers and dunlin, knot and redshanks, feeding, scocialising; clamorous at times, now quiet; plunging their beaks deep for cockles or lug worms. Flocks rose to wheel and twist and turn, to shower down, to run at speed, or to congregate in groups to await the sea's advance, so, that when it came and lessened the exposed banks they were forced to rise to fly over the water, calling plaintively, in protest, seeking drier refuge. Surging skiens of geese flew over, going south, clamorous, calling, one to each other, all the while. Here and there a solitary gaunt heron stood, more patient than any other bird, waiting for its food, sometimes for hours on end. Then, swift as a flash, its neck would shoot out to stab an unsuspecting fish, which has come too close. When it had fed it flies off to a new hunting place, kronking in triumph.

On the greensward, on the mainland, there was already gathered a considerable throng of people. Tents had been set up. Behind the Castle, in the deeper water, eight birlins rode at anchor, vessels, which had brought visitors by sea. A lone piper played the ancient composition, "The Chief's Welcome to Strath Appin".

With a loud shout Alasdair went off down the slope, on his garron, to greet young Rob Stewart, who was his friend of long standing. Iain, Alasdair's brother took his time. He wondered if Alasdair would see Fiona, the daughter of Ardshiel, to whom he was betrothed. As day drew into evening the Chiefs were rowed across the short width of water to Isle Stalker, whilst the rest of the assembly were left to entertain themselves, as best they could, on shore. Each Chief had brought his own personal gift for Appin; Lochiel brought a finely crafted dirk with a dark amethyst set in the hilt, which glowed in the flickering candle light ; Glengarry a silver quaich with gripping beast designs worked around its rim, Young Keppoch four fine cows, which had had to be left on the mainland; MacDougal a targe covered with bull hide and studded with brass bosses. MacIain tendered his, a roll of material, which, when the ties securing it were undone, fell open to show a tapestry sewn by his wife, Mary. It was a thing of beauty, depicting a fourteen-pointer Imperial. Head up, all in pride it stood. Many gasped for they could have reached out and stroked its back, it was so real, the nostrils distended as it sniffed the air, the Damh Mor, the Great Stag of legend. Amongst the company many there were who looked to see the high stepping hinds follow, such was the reality of it. Light seemed to touch its antlers and the points gleamed golden. Spontaneously applause broke out. With a slight bow to his uncle, Ardshiel, the Tutor, young Stewart of Appin took the cloth and walked the length of the hall, reached up to lift down a claymore, to hang the gift in its place. Mary would be pleased when told, MacIain knew. Where other women sewed with a dull and uninspiring needle, her creations were an art form; tiny and tight the threads. Each colour placed so that it was a foil to the other; thus, the cloth became vibrant and full of life, and the themes she composed had total meaning, with impact on the eye, a pleasure to behold.

"There will be a short interval, at which time if you care to take a turn outside there will be a surprise for all. I would thank you for being here and for the fine gifts ".

With no more ado there was a general exodus. Once all were without, a horn sounded; a fire arrow was shot from the Castle roof and, almost at once two bonfires flamed, one on Isle Shuna and one on the east end of the Island of Lismore. With panache Stewart's piper blew up and gave them in turn, "The Highland Punch Bowl", "The Thief of Lochaber" and "The Reel of the Blackcocks", the skirling music floating on the wind. It was agreed by all that it was, indeed, a good surprise.

Now, back in the hall, the feast began. They were served dried and salted lamb, hot and steaming, in golden bubbles, on a bed of birch twigs, together with dried fluke fish, which had been steeped in lye of hardwood ashes and water for three weeks, so, that when cooked and dished up it had an almost jelly like texture. There were farles of oatcackes and golden churn turned butter, all to be followed, as to be expected in Appin of the Deer, with collops of venison and wheaten loaves. There were great bowls of ale, from which one could quaff one's thirst, or if one chose, spirit from the two ankers of Cognac, which MacIain had provided, or Claret, rich and ruby red.

Afterwards, when the boards were cleared, the entertainment began. Musicians vied as to who was best, harpists, pipers and singers and the wordsmiths stood, in turn, to please the guests as they thought fit. Without doubt, Iain Lom, the Bard of Keppoch, renowned for his verses throughout Gaeldom, who could compile a satire, which could blast the reputation of a man, or, who could, turn to a total understanding of the birds and the beasts, or if he had a mind to it he could produce a description of a falling stream of water, in all its beauty, he was outstanding. His poem on The Battle of Inverlochy, to which he had guided Montrose, on the epic march prior to the engagement, was, in particular, pleasing to all the MacDonalds, MacDougal and the Stewarts who relished it's anti Campbell theme, having no love for them,

"Were you familiar with the Goirtean Odhar? Well was
it manured, not by the dung of sheep or goats, but by the
blood of Campbells after it had congealed".
Ending with the chilling lines:
"Perdition take you if I feel pity for your plight,
As I listen to the distress of your children,
Lamenting the company which was in the battlefield,
The wailing of the women of Argyll".

MacIain was delighted that his long time friend was so well received. With Iain Lom things blazed and burned. When he viewed a scene there was no black and white, only reds and greens and vibrant blues, and sometimes, away out on the edge of thought, was hard won gold. Gradually, as the night drew on the company thinned as the heavy meal and the drink took its toll. Many slept on the floor, whilst those of the High Chiefs, who could manage, climbed the stairs to go to bed in one of the upper chambers.

Dawn came, few were up and about. Out, before the castle rock, the waters of Loch Linnhe were a hundred shades of blue; a lovely, gentle light flooded the ramparts of the mountains, where mist folded and moved, refolded ands moved again, in a pearl grey sky. Wisps hung, veil-like, caught between rock cliffs, and, all on high was drifting purple and silver grey.

Many had gone off to hunt deer, and indeed MacIain would have preferred that, knowing that in Luath and Bran he had deerhounds which could out run and out last any other man's dogs, but, to humour his sons, he had agreed to go with them to watch young Stewart fly his falcons at grouse.

They went up on to the rise of ground to the west of the House of Achnacone, below the Brown Hill, where, if you looked back, there was a wonderful view of Castle Stalker, framed in a pronounced vee of the land, The dogs were loosed, whose purpose was to flush the birds. Birches stood, caught in their own fire of green, the leaves holding the light in a glory of translucency. Young Stewart stripped the hood from the falcon's head and let the noble eyes take the light. She sat there, on her masters gloved arm, proud and fierce; her upper parts slate grey with dark bars, black moustached; the

85

curved bill horn-blue; the eyes distant points of fire. Quickly, but with gentleness, Stewart tossed the bird up into the wind. She rose, climbing in a narrow spiral, wafting a thousand feet higher with unhurried ease; a lyrical quality about her going. Sunlight touched the underside of her wings and the cream and brown surfaces were silvered. She paused to drift, then swept up into smallness. Long winged, lean and powerful. Her being was filled with joy, for, she, like all of her kind, loved the wind, for only in it did she truly live; to her, the sun and the rush of the air and the purity of the all embracing sky. Effortlessly she glided over the land. With a suddenness she rose, lifting up on the rim of a cloud, dark and crozzled with dappled sun -shadow, floating on it, veering and swaying from side to side in careless freedom, in a rush of air. Wind streamed from the curve of her wings. Like a transient beam of sunlight she flashed across the clouds.

Below, absorbed, the watching people identified with the bird, but they knew, that, as hunters, they were her inferiors. Beneath her the earth poured away. Ceaseley, she scanned it with small abrupt turns of her head, the retinas of her eyes recording objects twice more acutely than the human eye ----- There was movement below, immediately the cells in the foveal area of her eyes focussed, and that which moved, flared like crimson flame, into larger, clearer view, with a resolution eight times better than that of the human eye. Five grouse came flying fast and true for their chosen destination. Four were in a tight group, the fifth was out on the flank, detached.

There was no mistaking the falcon's first easy drifting fall. She banked left, feeling for winghold on the sweep of the sky. Of a sudden she poured down in vertical descent. For a thousand feet she dropped, her wings flung up and back, like the flights of a hurtling arrow. Her claws opened, gleaming golden. Down she went, through the sunlight. Air hissed sibilantly as she passed through it. In a blur she hit the chosen bird ----- the needle talons drove in ----- death bloomed ----- and it was slain. With a dull thud the earth came up to meet the body, to give it final totality.

Above a tiny puff of feathers floated, hanging, waiting to be winnowed by the wind.

XVIII. The Advocate.

Cognisant of the intolerance shown to Catholics, but being also of a mind to allow every man to worship as he saw fit, coupled with the fact that religious strife was ruining trade and prosperity, James decided that, central to his view of Kingship, conscience ought not to be forced. Therefore, he introduced the Declaration of Indulgence. He was stunned by the fury, which erupted, from all and sundry. The Catholics were quiet on the subject, perhaps having most to gain, though they were only a very small minority. Most acrimonious of all were the loyalist Episcopalians and the moderate Presbyterians, both of whom had suffered at the hands of the fanatical Western Fundamentalists. To them the King seemed to be arranging for them to go back to their old ways. Of a certainty, the dykes in Holland would be breached and the exiled zealots would flood in to Scotland. No loyal majority could countenance a welcome extended to the Scarlet Woman or the Suffering Remnant.

Courageously, Balcarres wrote to James – "The terror of bringing back a party, who have ever lain at catch, for the bringing down of the Monarchy, and had cost your predecessors much time, blood and treasure, to humble; made even your firmest and faithfullest servants comply with your demands, but with an unwilling mind".

Like a spent cannon ball the King's popularity plunged. At the meetings of the Privy Council discussion rose to white heat.

Sir George Mackenzie, the Lord Advocate, was asked to reason with James, for it was recognised that as the presenter of an argument he had few equals. His, the gift, to be able to put more meaning in any one sentence than others could speak in a day. Words had always been his best weapon. When he began his voice was soft, a trick of his. He would commence so quietly that one had to strain to hear him, and, as he outlined his idea, his voice would rise until it resonnated like a beaten drum, but with a strange intensely musical lilt, with the "r's" of his speech rolling like a tambour.

His talent came to nothing for the King sat frozen faced, letting Sir George's words beat like icy rain on his ears.

"As King, mine is the right to decide, there will be no turning on this matter. Should there be those who cannot accept my decision then they must thole it". With that the King rose from his seat, dismissal in every line of him. The audience was over.

Four days later Mackenzie sent his letter of resignation, as Lord Advocate, to His Majesty. He was unable, he wrote, to thole the Toleration Scheme, as it was constituted.

Cognisant of the fact that he could not do without a Kings Advocate James cast about for a replacement. Swiftly he appointed Sir John Dalrymple. Dundee, amongst others, was disturbed. How could his King, his erst-while friend, the past Duke of York, accept the going of Sir George Mackenzie and replace him with a turn-coat, a capricious opportunist, a trimmer, a man, whose father would not take the Test, and who had flown the country, to go to Holland, to consort with Argyll and his like? Whose Mother was a rabid Conventicler, who had been friend to Peden and other rebels? Dundee and many others could find no answer. God save the King!

Seven months later, James, realising the mistake he had made, in that Mackenzie was better suited to the position, being honest to a fault, more attuned to events, more skilled in the arts of diplomacy, more of a man of the people, had him reinstated as King's Advocate. Dalrymple was relegated to the position of Justice Clerk.

XIX. THE KING'S ADIEU.

Rumours abounded, spread far and wide. The pregnant Queen was not pregnant, and the child to be born to her would be a changeling. Soon the King was to massacre the Protestants. The Scarlet Woman of Catholicism would come into her own. Rome would rule the Realm.

At this time the King recalled the British Regiments serving in the Low Countries, but the States General refused to release them.

Melfort persuaded James that the forces in Scotland should be sent to augment the English Army against the threatened invasion by William of Orange. This alarmed Claverhouse greatly. He penned a letter, in vain, to the King, to persuade him otherwise, informing him that the malcontents, in Scotland, would seize on the chance so presented; Melford had his agents suppress the dispatch.

In October two thousand seven hundred men, under the Command of Douglas, marched south, Drummond's Dragoons, Douglas's Foot Guards, Buchannan's Regiment and Claverhouse's Horse.

Lean and hollow, the theologians, with faces like platefuls of venial sin, immediately swarmed into Edinburgh. They were on every street, the epitome of godliness, with heads bowed in devotion, but what were their thoughts? Wondrous hot for religion, whipped up to white heat. From pulpits, at street corners, from the widows of the tenements, out over the people rolled the thunder of denunciation, a litany of hate. James, the King, was referred to as "The sworn vassal of the Anti Christ" and Roman Catholicism as "The Kingdom of Darkness". Passages from the Bible were seized upon and interpreted to the Preachers' fancy. Eccleastes three, seventeen, was a favourite – "God will judge the righteous and the wicked, for he has appointed a time for every matter and for every work". Another was "You shall go forth in the name of the Lord God, who has sworn to deliver mine enemies into mine hand". Triumphant and vocal the black clothed men, in clerical garb, brought business in the town to a standstill.

In good order the Scottish army arrived in London, having marched south by way of Carlisle and Preston. Claverhouse had gone on ahead. Much to his surprise, when he arrived, the King chose this, the time, to announce his elevation to the Scottish Peerage as Viscount Dundee and Lord Graham of Claverhouse, in recognition of the many services done on behalf of King Charles the Second and his Majesty, King James by the trusty Major General John Graham.

Privately, in conversation with Dundee, James intimated that no honour was more deserved, for his loyalty alone, which he described as " persistent and true".

"You have given of yourself selflessly. Of all our subjects none can match you or surpass you in duty. Would that all, or even a few, were as you. Despite wealth, honours and favour enjoyed, we are hedged about by base men, who will ever be base. James, you are more to me than a friend, you are a rock, steadfast in an ocean surging with waves of envy and deceit, which casts up, at each tide, a tangle of vegetation, to lie upon the pristine beach of our land, to rot and decay, and to foul the very air with its loathsome stench".

Early in November, aided by a fair wind, William of Orange landed at Torbay, with his polyglot army. It comprised, amongst others of a squadron of feather decked Negroes, the Anglo-Scots Brigade, Danes, Finns in jet black armour and a strong force of French Huguenots. They marched, under the watchful eye of General Hugh Mackay, to Exeter, where they quartered. With the King came men who had fled earlier who had been unable to take the Test, or who were political refugees; amongst them John Cochrane and John Dalrymple.

Commanded by the Earl of Feversham the army took up position at Salisbury, where the King, on arrival, found it to be in disarray. Each morning troops had gone missing, deserting under the cover of night. Worse, senior Officers were defecting. Amongst them, the most prominent, was Major General John Churchill, a bastard son of Charles the Second.

As if in a trance the King swiftly returned to London, lethargic, not wishing to take advice, in a dreamlike state, which those who knew him found difficult to comprehend. For, this was the man of action, of whom the Great Marshall Turene had said, "if I were to try to conquer the World I would have my army led by the Duke of York". This was the man who had led the Navy to defeat the Dutch, who had inspired officers and men in the teeth of War.

That his son-in-law could invade and threaten he could not comprehend. This was compounded, more sorely, when he learnt that his daughter, the Princess Anne and her husband had gone to join William. No longer able to contain himself he burst into tears. "God help me, my children forsake me".

With no more ado, broken by his family's desertion the King ordered the army to be disbanded. In despair he crossed the Thames, at Vauxhall, throwing the great seal of England into the river, on his way to France and exile.

XX. The Mall.

At Balcarres suggestion a meeting was called, of any of the Privy Council available, to take place in the London house of the Duke of Hamilton. Balcarres, Lord Livingstone, Old Airlie and General Douglas were present. There was much doubt in Dundee's mind as to the loyalty of both Douglas and Hamilton. Already Dundee had been approached by Douglas suggesting he should defect, but as Dundee had been sworn to secrecy he was unable to raise the point.

At the table Hamilton presided. There were carafes of Malmsey, decanters of Claret and jugs of dark brown malt Porter set around for anyone to sample as they so chose. Balcares produced a letter from the Council in Scotland.

Hamilton demanded to have it in his hand but Balcarres refused to give it up, which provoked a great row, with the Duke, who was in high dudgeon and full of bluster. Collin remained calm. Eventually, the meeting was over, the participants going their various ways without anything having been decided.

Three days later, to the amazement of all, sensation of sensations, the King was back in town! His journey to France had been aborted, due to a chain of hitches.

As he made his way to St.James's he was feted by the crowd, which had turned out to see him. Church bells were rung and bonfires were lit in celebration at his return.

With his spirits uplifted the King sent word to William proposing that they meet in conference, at St.James's Palace. Out of hand William spurned the offer.

Some of his Generals came to James and asked that they should be permitted to reassemble the disbanded troops, but the King refused to authorise the recall.

Hoping to cheer James and to show their support Balcarres and Dundee called on the King. They were taken a back by his appearance, he had lost weight and now had a gaunt, haggard look, and seemed hesitant and uncertain. His eyes were like blank windows in a darkened room.

"Let us walk", said the King. So, off they sauntered along the Mall. Wind came from the west, not strong but persistent, shaking the bare limbs of the leafless lime trees. Overhead, legs trailing, wings slow as heart- beats, a single heron flew. To the left, on the grassland, a clamour of gorged rooks cawed in protest as they lifted from the ground. From an upper branch a magpie yabbered obscenities.

"Your Majesty", said Balcarres, "The army will rise for you at once, let us call it".

"Do not presume too much, my friends. Already there are those who have forsaken me, men I once trusted to the full, close kin, blood of my blood. Why do you two remain steadfast?"

"Sire, we are both agreed that we would never find a better master than yourself, and neither of us will ever change our allegiance", replied Dundee.

For several minutes they walked on unspeaking, with only the sound of the breeze and black rooks calling.

At last the King spoke. "Never the less, I am decided. I can never be a prisoner of the upstart William. My intention is to join the Queen in France. For the future, come what may, I will authorise commissions for your appointments, you Balcarres to be responsible for the handling of the Civil Affairs of Scotland, and my Lord Dundee to be elevated to be Commander – in – Chief of the Scottish Army, with the rank of Major General".

There was little more to be said. So, the three men walked back to the Palace, in silent moments of sad pain. To each theirs and theirs alone, to be borne and felt in all its poignancy, sorrow unbending, bitter to bear.

With abruptness William sent his Dutch Guard to Whitehall. At the King's order the Coldstream Guard stood down. For the night the Sovereign was guarded by foreign troops. At one of the morning, before the cocks ever crowed, James was wakened from his bed by three emissaries from William, who informed him, without ceremony, but with courtesy, that he must leave London that morning.

Again, the King went down river, in his barge, rowed by his Watermen, to take ship to France. Salt tears ran down his face, unhindered, to gather at the angles of his jaw, until gravity and the wind teased them free. In to his brain, unsought, from Richard the Second, by Will Shakespear, came the words – "Mine honour is my life, both grow in one. Take honour from me and my life is done".

In great magnificence William of Orange, that afternoon, processed to St. James's Palace.

In England there was no precedent for a peaceful coup-de-tat or for the replacement of a living Monarch, against his will, by constitutional means, in particular by a person with no natural right of succession. What to do? A Convention was held in February, but no decision was come to as to how to fill the throne. Unbidden, William, himself, supplied the answer. Categorically, he stated, that he would not rule as Regent, only as King. If the Convention did not award the crown jointly to himself and the Princess Mary, they could stew in their own juice, he would simply quit England and return to Holland!

Towards the end of the month the Princess Mary came to England and the Convention tendered the crown, which was formally accepted.

There were Scotsmen, in the main of Presbyterian persuasion, many of them who had fled to Holland earlier, with Stair to the fore and the Duke of Hamilton, who met with William at St. James's. He proposed to them that they should present a solution for governing Scotland. They responded by intimating that they would similarly hold a Convention in Edinburgh, in March, to debate the matter. In the interim they asked that William assume the administration of the Kingdom.

Reeling from recent events, Dundee, fretting at the inaction of sitting in camp, wrote to William to ask if he could take his troops back north? As was his wont, never one for hiding the truth, he also added that he could not be party to the removal of his rightful Ruler.

The reply came swiftly. You may do so wrote William, informing him that he would be under his protection provided he lived peacefully, at home, on his estates.

Thanking him Dundee responded by saying he would live in peace, unless he was forced to do otherwise.

Early, on a grey February morning Dundee mounted up his dragoons, and in company with Balcarres, took forty or so of the best cavalry, in Europe, away north, for Dudhope.

XXI. The Glen.

In three years Mary had never been higher up the Glen than at Loch Achtriochtan. Now at last MacIain was taking her. She was more excited than she had been for weeks. They had spent the night with Achtriochtan and his wife, old friends together. Her husband had been careful to see that he did not have too much to drink, for they were risen early and were away on the garrons, in the darkness, so that they would be in place, on the skirts of Rannoch Moor before daybreak.

They had halted, still in darkness on the north bank of the River Coupal to await the coming of day. Slowly, imperceptibly the land appeared as the night drained away and shapes began to emerge. The sunrise was a thing of immeasurable loveliness. Before them Buachaille Etive Mor, the Great Shepherd of Etive, took form, bathed in the rich pink glow of dawn, an arrow head, and as the sun touched it its porphyry rock, before one's eyes, took on its own unique rich collation of rose, with, here and there, a deep red and incandescent amber. All was living light on blood-wine rock, pared to the elemental bone, a sculpture, chiselled by time, to God's glory. At that instant, to Mary and MacIain, the landscape was theirs and theirs alone.

There was little cloud and, as the morning went on the sky became robin egg blue. Looking away east, out over the vastness of Rannoch, an immutable empty solitude of desolation, they could just see, almost at the limit of sight, mountains rising ethereal, with amongst them the perfect cone of Schiehallion, the Fairy Hill. For her part Mary was entranced for never before had she looked on such a primitive, raw place, totally untouched by man, pathless and untrodden.

As she turned Buachaille Etive Mor, with total impact on the eye, sprang from the great sea-moss of Rannoch.

Now it was time to make their way back into the Glen, down past the old coffin cairns. As they came into the throat of the Pass, where the track fell steeply, Mary waited, wondering if what her husband's sons had told her of would happen? And it did, MacIain dismounted from his horse and led it by the reins. "He always, on his return, will walk, for, he avers that, at the lip of Glencoe it whispers to him, like no other place, and that the pulse of the land rises through the soles of his feet and that his spirit walks with his ancestors, right back to Iain Abrach, the first MacDonald Chief of the Glen".His land underfoot, the song of the wind as it blew through the pass, the souls of the hills, the laughter of running waters. Then, they were at the fall where the Allt Lairig Eilde joined the Coe. Mary marvelled at it, even though her husband told her that in time of spate it was much more awesome. For sixty feet the water fell, in a ceaseless twin branch. As it came over the lip of the land it described a pronounced arc to pour down into a run of lesser falls, which flowed from one inky pot to the next, the river tumbling down, a wild mass of water coursing over time worn rock, its voice never still, its colours ever changing, topaz, citrine, smoky-quartz, and creamy curded foam.

As they descended the gorge of the River Coe, which lay before them, secretive, deep cut, with fast rapids, slow glides, dark unlit places, and unexpectedly, on the terraces and shelves of Aonach Dubh, where goats and cattle could not graze, were beautiful miniature trees, birch, scarlet-berried mountain ash, holly, oaks, willows and dark needled red-barked pines with knarled rock grasping roots.

Where the river entered Loch Achtriochtan there was a hundred-yard long, irregular triangular shaped scree of boulders, strewn in a random pattern, which the next spate would alter, at its will. At their approach a heron lifted off from its midst, with deceptively indolent wing beats, its legs atrail. It disappeared into the distance, indifferent, aloof, leaving behind it an intimation of disdain.

At summer level the Loch was much smaller in area, than Mary recalled. To her regret there were no yellow nosed swans. However, there were ducks aplenty, with mallard, teal and a pair of elegant pintail

"You see The Three Sisters", said MacIain, "In winter for five months they lie in shade, never knowing the touch of sun. Some call them the Sisters of Shadow".

But, now in light, They rose, omnipresent, heights of heaped and fractured rock, spilling black buttresses of frozen stone, earthwards, in ancient, pleated curtains, laconic, yet subject to natures whims, to do with as she willed.

To the north the great mountain wall of Aonach Eagach rose, hundreds of feet high, sheer, nacreous, awe inspiring, with streams of boulders down its face. On its very top a hail shower drifted, before the west wind, palest silver, floating, hauntingly lovely, insubstantial, and then, of a sudden, it was gone. Glencoe's weather, as always, was contemptuous, unique, and it's alone.

After the great limitless Moss of Rannoch the hills of the Glen hedged all about as no other mountains ever could.

At the clachan of Achtriochtan they were made hugely welcome. All of the women knew Mary from her visits, for, from the beginning, she had made a point, in company with Achtriochan's wife, of going to each house, in turn, spending time with the occupants, sewing with the women, speaking with the aged and doing what she could for the sick. MacIain and his cousin, Achtriochan, had a glass of whisky each. All of the bards, who lived there, wanted the Chief to hear the latest verse they had composed, but MacIain, not wishing to offend, told them that he would return in a week's time to listen to them.

It was hard to get away, but eventually they did so, riding off on the garrons for their summer house in Glen Leac-na-Muidhe. Soon, very soon, it would be time to shut the house up and move to their winter dwelling of Polvaig, at Invercoe.

They came up round the long curve of the glen, with its unbroken flank, mountains all about, then it veered a away before them to the steep rise up to the Pass. Aonach Eagach masked the north, Bidean and Aoanach Dubh a' Chlinne held the east in subjection, Creag Bhan to the west and Sgor na h-Ulaidh hemmed it in, whilst Meal Mor stood, full-square, at the mouth, as if daring mere men to enter.

At the door of their house they paused, before going in, to watch the coming of night. Slowly, as the sun dropped, clouds caught fire above the jagged silhouettes of the peaks, declivities filled with deep purple. Saffron flashed and shades of carmine, and delicate pinks stole in, whilst, imperceptibly, the shadows melded into night and all the land was shrouded in darkness. Stars lit till all the heavens were bejewelled with golden constellations. This was the hour of mystery, when the past and the future clasped hands across the fleeting present and time-touched things were made anew.

XXII. THE CONVENTION.

Meltford, whom Dundee considered to be incompetent, had fled the country, even before James. Perth, the Chancellor, languished in Kirkcaldy jail. Queensberry was at home, uncommitted, whilst his brother Douglas and his son Drumlanrigg had become staunch supporters of William. Sir George Mackenzie, having used all of his oratorical skills to persuade the Privy Council not to send a message of welcome to William was unlikely to remain as the Lord Advocate for much longer. For the time being Scotland was ruled by the Duke of Hamilton, who, to strengthen his hand, had filled Edinburgh with his followers from Clydesdale, who swaggered, armed, throughout the town.

His wife being near her time Dundee remained, at Dudhope, awaiting the birth of their first child. In company with Balcarres Dundee composed a draft letter, dignified, conciliatory, and in no way presumtive, which they forwarded to James, in France, asking for his permission to present it, bearing the King's signature, to the Convention, which had been called for the fourteenth of March. For, privately, they did not consider that Melfort had the nous to write something suitable.

It was almost impossible to find accommodation in Edinburgh, the town was thronged with people come for the Convention, or to do associated business. Many of the Lords had brought armed followers with them for their personal protection. The air was charged with raw excitement. Rumours were abroad of a plot to assassinate Sir George Mackenzie and Dundee.

Fuelled by pride, a half mocking, deprecating smile on his lips, with an unspeakable arrogance about him, the Duke of Hamilton chaired the meeting. On the first day discussion and argument, as to procedure, took up most of the time. Of Greatest import, the matter of Edinburgh Castle still being held by the Duke of Gordon, in the name of King James, was raised. It was resolved that the Duke be summoned, forthwith, to surrender to the Convention. Surreptitiously, Balcarres and Dundee had a note smuggled into the Castle, which stiffened the resolve of the Custodian to continue to hold out, even though he had been on the point of complying.

In the night, at great risk, Dundee made his way into the fortress and in discussion with the elderly Duke gave him new heart to carry on his resistance.

Next day the Convention was aghast at the refusal to give the Castle up. John Dalrymple, the Master of Stair, stole a glance at Dundee's face, which remained impassive, he wondered if his enemy of old had anything to do with the turn of events? Straightaways, the gloriously dressed Heralds, in blues, reds and gold were instructed to proceed to the Castle foreground, there to blow their trumpets and to declare Gordon outlaw, which they did to the derisory jeers of the garrison.

When Sir George Mackenzie laid documents before the Assembly, which were evidence of the plot to kill Dundee and himself, in his element, dressed in slate grey broadcloth and a gleaming white stock, Dalrymple rose to his feet. Totally adept at turning an opportunity into something that would meet his objective under the smokescreen of legal process he ruled that "public affairs cannot be postponed in order to consider private matters".

"Surely, this matter is of the public domain?" Sir George interjected.

With the line of a smile at his mouth ready to continue Dalrymple was about to speak. He need not have bothered, for Hamilton pounded on the table with his gavel and ruled that the Convention must carry on with other pressing business.

Crane, one of the Queen's servants had brought the letter from James in France. It was agreed that it should be read.

"However", intoned Hamilton, "William, Prince of Orange, has also written to the Convention, I propose it be read first".

No one demurred.

When the contents of William's letter had been heard Crane

was called upon to read out King James's. Like a thunderclap, the words fell into the vaulted silence of Parliament House, washing over it in a flood of bombast. The beat of them was like icy rain, falling on Collin Llindsay, Earl of Balcarres and Dundee's ears; the sentences and their meaning as chilling as the deep cold of winter on the hills. Almost at once they recognised the style of Melfort. Both felt the agony of defeat, the very depth of despair, as stupid, arrogant, threatening language brazenly sounded forth. At last it ended, There was no way that Dundee and Balcarres could admit that they had told the King what he should write. They knew that in the act of its reading it would give the throne of Scotland to William.

Later, much later, it emerged that Melfort had prevented the messenger from meeting the King, and had dealt with the matter himself.

That evening many meetings, formal or informal took place in Edinburgh, those for William and those for James. It was the decision of those for the King to move to Stirling, to hold their own Convention there.

XXIII. EDINBURGH.

There was a decided chill in the air, a rising mist was seeping off the River Forth, its thin fingers reaching and groping, like a lost soul's, clutching in vain, to find a hold. Horses snorted steam from there nostrils. As they bucked and danced their equipment jingled and rattled. With a careless ease Dundee swung up into the saddle and at once man and beast were as one.

Most who had said they would come were there, with the notable exception of Collin Lindsay, Earl of Balcarres and Athol. However, Dundee did not let it faze him, for he had made his mind up, the night before, that he would leave the Capital, come what may.

His Troop was there, some of the best and most highly trained cavalry in Europe, loyal to a man. The command rang out and the mounted cavalcade moved off amidst a gallant clatter of hooves. On high, from a window, Collin Lindsay watched, wanting to go, his mind full of doubts.

Past the Weigh House, down the West Bow they went. The horses' hooves scliffing on the cobbles. Along the Cowgate, exiting at its Port, turning north by Leith Wynd, past the Netherbow Port and Trinity Hospital, with the rising mass of Saltoun Crags to the left, until they reached the Lang Dykes, which they swung into, to go due west.

Above them, dominating, the Castle stood, reared up on its volcanic plug of fire formed rock. At its foot the Nor Loch lay, its waters inky black, still and unmoving, until catspaws of wind sent tiny waves tripping across its surface, so that, in places, it sparkled as if someone had scattered pinches of silver dust, which took the light, just for the minutest instant, and made it visual, the scene magic, imprinting itself upon the retina of the mind. Just as suddenly the wind died and the waters lay unmoving, totally still, dark and enigmatic.

Near to the Church of St.Cuthbert Dundee halted them. Curtly he bade all dismount and to wait till he returned. Unaccompanied he made his way to the base of the Castle crag and slowly but purposefully began to ascend, making his way upwards to the postern gate, which was set in the north- eastern face of the rock. By now townspeople had gathered to watch him climb, shouting words of encouragement, even though many of them had no idea of the identity of the man they championed.

At the gate Dundee was met by the Duke of Gordon, whose face was filled with tension lines.

"Back again", observed the Duke.

"Your Grace, matters of great importance, myself and those men who are for King James have quit the Convention. We go to Stirling to hold our own meeting to decide how best to give support. However, for yourself, for whom the holding of the Castle is indeed critical, and a deed, which reflects your steadfastness, in the face of all adversity, there is truly news of great moment. King James has landed in Ireland, with an army and intends, after his presence there, has been established, to send reinforcements to Scotland, which, with the forces for him here, will ensure victory over the usurper".

"Indeed, Dundee, that is heartening. Perhaps, 'tis best we cut the talk short, for I have no doubt there will be those who would seek to apprehend you or may even wish to do you harm".

"I ask your Grace that you banish any timorousness and any irresolution you may harbour. A bold heart is half the battle; the only thing that grows over time is the reputation of those who have lived honourably. Should you cede the fortress tomorrow you would do so with esteem, in mens eyes, for, you have held it with purpose against all odds. Hold it longer for our King".

With that, the two men embraced. Dundee, stepped back, with care, to salute the Duke with military precision, and, at once set off on the climb down

Suddenly, there was an uncalled for interruption to the proceedings. A man had burst in to the Parliament Hall, past the guards, sucking in lungfulls of air. Breathlessly, he panted out, "The

Lord Dundee is up the rock, talking to Gordon over the Castle wall".

There was a stunned silence. Then a welling rise of voices as all gathered tried to make their points of view heard. Havoc ensued. Hamilton reacted first, sending off a messenger to alert his followers, throughout the town, calling them to meet, armed, at St.Giles Kirk. Train- bands were called out. Drums were beat and church bells rung. Panic flowed along the streets of the city.

To late, by far, the Convention sent a messenger after Dundee, to call on him to return and explain what he intended. He was long gone, at a stiff trot, well on the way to Linlithgow. The messenger never did catch up with him

With apparent delight, next day, in the Parliament Hall, Dalrymple moved that Dundee be declared "Outlaw". So, it was resolved, with a price of five thousand pounds, dead or alive, be put on his head. Later Dalrymple was to raise this to the unheard of sum of twenty thousand pounds.

In all their ancient and glorious panoply of reds and blues and gold the Heralds put the Viscount Dundee, Lord James Graham, to the horn, at the Mercat Cross of Edinburgh and two days later repeated the anathema at the cross in Dundee.

XXIV. CRIEFF.

There was a great bustle in the town. Drovers had brought their cattle from all over the Highlands, as they had done for many years, to Crieff, for the last sale of the year. All about cows were stanced, with dogs attempting to ensure they did not stray into someone else's herd. Men ran about clouting beasts across their quarters to bring them into line. Stallholders called out to attract trade. Here and there a piper played. Taverns, everywhere did a roaring business. Barmaids were run off their feet; innkeepers were trying, as best they could, to keep order, whilst attempting not to upset customers.

Near, where the bridge crossed the River Earn, was a favourite inn of the drovers, The Black Grouse. Once they had passed under its swinging painted sign, the tired and thirsty men were in a different world. Inside it was packed with people, hot with the heat of their bodies, the air foetid, overlain with the overpowering smell of ale. Conversation rippled, scraps of gossip, of rumour, the prices of cattle, the state of trade. Old friends, who had probably not met for a year, shouted out greetings, across the room. Beer mugs clinked. There was an incessant hubbub.

Each evening six Highlanders came to the table reserved for them by the inn- keeper, to play at cards. The game was Ombre. Three men played for a given time, then two dropped out, and two others took their places. So it went, turn on turn, to ensure that all had a chance to play. Three of them were good, perhaps, better than good. When these three were opposed a crowd would gather round to watch. By the night's end, though the stakes played for were not high, usually, one of the three finished up with the pot.

On the second night, as the game progressed, a stranger entered, with two companions. He was a big man, well built, radiating power, in middle age, just starting to go bald. At his neck was a jabot, a white waterfall of lace. His eyes were small, close set, the face weather beaten. He was neat and tidy, scrubbed clean, his beard trimmed, his fingernails cut short. As time passed, from the crowd's talk, it was learnt that this was Arthur Stoneywood, one of the richest dealers in cattle, in the country; buying from the Clansmen and selling on into England.

Hand after hand the game went on, until only the three best players were left. Having drunk several measures of ale and a quarter gill of brandy Stoneywood began to comment on the game, more and more insistently, until several of the onlookers called on him to hold his tongue, but he glared at them, and would not. Then he reached out and took the ace of spades, the Spadille, the highest trump card, from the fingers of one of the players, and flicked it onto the table.

"There you are", he exclaimed. "Beat that"

"First, Sir, it is unforgivable to interfere with a game, in play", said one of the Highlanders. "Second you do not understand the game, for I had no intention of playing that ace, having no other trumps, I can play any card"

With no apparent haste the Clansman rose, with his eyes close to Stoneywood's, unwavering, with just the faintest hint of a smile on his lips.

"Never do that again"

"So the dog barks", said the Cattle Dealer.

"If need be it will bite".

Quickly, sensing trouble, the inn-keeper moved in and with his helpers had Stoneywood shepherded away.

For two nights more the Highlanders played undisturbed. On the third evening Stoneywood appeared. From the outset he seemed bent on trouble. To start with he began making comments on the game. Tension built in the room. Play went on, the Clansmen seemingly unconscious of his presence. Then came the fateful moment when the Cattle Dealer lent over to touch a card on the table.

In a single instant one of the tartan clad men reached to his left armpit and drew an oxter knife from its sheath. His eyes narrowed to slits, then they came fully open, filled with flame. In a fluid flow of motion he drove the knife down through Stoneywood's hand, pining it to the table. The Dealer screamed, his blood pooling on the board, to temper the heat of the honed steel, his eyes widening in horror, as, in disbelief, he saw the ever-reddening surface.

Many there averred that they had never seen a knife strike like it. One present contended that, in speed and power, it had all of the attributes of a serpent's.

With athletic grace the Highlander rose, donned his bonnet, all the while holding the injured man's eyes with his own.

"You may keep the skian dubh seeing you hold it fast. Perhaps you will learn to be better mannered in the future". The words hung in the air, raw and tender as a bruise. Then he turned on his heel and led his companions out of the inn.

"Who was yon?" someone asked.

"That was himself, MacIain, the Chief man of Glencoe. It is fortunate, I am thinking, that the black rage did not come on him, and he showed restraint, or he might have put the skian elsewhere".

XXV. THE CRADLE.

Gulls rose in a huge calling throng, beating across the sky in a discordant clamour, the world filled with their noise, like whirling chaff thrown up by the flail. There was little wind. Any there was came fitfully from the west. Above the sun tried, with little success, to break through the clouds, but it did not rain. Drawn up before the House of Dudhope was Dundee's troop, tricked out in their very best uniforms, all on foot, for they did not want their horses to dig up the lawn.

As Dundee and the Lady Jean came out of the front door his brother gave the command, "General's Salute, present arms".

With precision the swords were unsheathed and swung up to the vertical, hilts to chins, the points skyward, where they were held for a brief moment, then brought down to be replaced in their scabbards.

"Troop ready for inspection", barked the Coronet David.

Whereupon, the Commander left his wife and proceeded to review his soldiers. At the finish he was escorted to the front of the men to where an object lay on the grass, swaddled in a white sheet.

"Permission to call on the Lady Jean to come up?"

"Granted", called out Dundee.

With dignity she came forward to take up position, a lady to her very core

" The Troop would be pleased if the Commander – in – Chief and the Lady Jean would accept this gift". David reached down and pulled the sheet off.

There was a momentary hush, in which the only sound was the croodling of pigeons on their perches on the stone ledges of the house. Then Dundee's wife clapped her hands in delight. "It is truly beautiful", she said. And it was.

For here before them lay a cradle of beech wood with oak rockers. Arcading graced the top of both the headboard and footboard, with vertical splats, festooned with dangling foliage, coming in from the edges. Below the round topped arches, on the headboard was a deep cut cartouche with the initials JC and JG worked into it, that of the husband and wife, and on the footboard a roundel, which contained a thistle; all of the vigorous carving was in high relief. Beneath, the rockers, which had been hand sawn from a two- inch thick plank of oak, had fluting on the curve.

"This is for yourself, Sir, and her Ladyship, in honour of the birth of your son"

About to speak Dundee held back, for Jean said it all for him.

"This we will treasure, for the kindness you all have shown us. It is truly splendid. My son will enjoy it."

With a great shout the dragoons drew of their bonnets and waved them in the air. Formed up once again they marched off to the beat of "Dumbarton's Drums".

That night, in bed, Jean asked her husband where had his wild soldiers found a cabinet- maker of such skill?

So, he told her.

"Many years ago, when I had only been in Galloway for a short time, a woman brought a boy to me, asking that he be taken on as a soldier. My Sergeant was very hostile, mainly due to the lad having one leg two inches shorter than the other, which made him walk with a corkscrew motion. Due to the mother's entreaties that, all of his life, he had wanted "to be a sojer", and, an unfathomable quality about the lad, a compound of pride, acceptance of what life had given him, and, on questioning, a good knowledge of horses, I had him enlisted. Quickly, it became apparent that Arnot, for that was his name, was a find indeed. However, just as quickly he lost his name, becoming "Fixer", for he could just about repair or renew anything, whether it be made of leather, metal or wood. Broken traces were riveted, new spokes spliced into wagon- wheels, or, if a man so wished, a new piece of equipment was made. Also if a horse was sick or injured he could tend it better than any veterinary, which endeared him to the men. On enquiring how he had learned the skills he possessed, he replied, "nae body taught me, a jist watched and minded how it wis done". Where he ever saw anyone work wood with delicacy I can't say, but he and he alone made the cradle".

What gave him the greatest pleasure was that his brother, David, who had missed his wedding, was in attendance.

XXVI. The Highland Reel.

Now, His Grace, the Duke of Hamilton and Dalrymple, were masters of all. There was nothing to stay for after the reading of the "King's letter". The King's cause was lost. Had not Major General Mackay, one of William's greatest commanders arrived at the port of Leith, with the Scots Brigade, battle hardened, famed for their discipline? The Convention had at its disposal armed forces, the Rebels had none.

Dundee pondered on this. If men were to rise for James they would be found in the Highlands. Montrose, his distant kinsman had, thirty years before, raised an army for the Stuarts. As an act of defiance and as a rallying call he raised the King's standard on Dundee Law. Then he took his troop north, into the unknown, into the trackless waste of mountains, rivers, lochs and immense, desolate bogs, where the writ of southeron government did not run. First he chose to go to Gordon country, perhaps as a result of his friendship with the Duke, who held the Castle, but more particularly because the Gordons, unlike any other Clan, had discovered the use of cavalry and put it to good purpose to give them control of a huge swathe of territory from Findhorn Bay to Banff, fenced in by the Hills of Cromdale and the Ladder Hills. To have even a hundred Gordon Horse would be superb.

When not on horseback Dundee's time was taken up with letter writing. Each evening he would pen his correspondence, working long into the night. In the morning it was despatched, to be carried by a member of his own Troop, to the Laird or Clan Chief he thought might furnish warriors.

They marched and counter marched. It was a time of great learning for John Graham. He had to deal with Clan jealousies,

Chiefs in stiff- necked pride, waverers, who had to be persuaded, food shortages, the perpetual lack of money. There were other things he had to come to accept, the return home by Clan members when booty was taken; a practice as old as time, immutable. At one point he saw his force drop from nine hundred to six hundred when the Keppoch MacDonalds went off with the cattle they had lifted from the Mackintosh lands.

General Mackay had come in pursuit, but by dint of Dundee having better intelligence and each never knowing exactly where the other was, they did not meet, though on several occasion they passed closely. Letters came from Ireland, none from King James, all from Meltford's hand. They were as nothing to Dundee. He treated them as if they were balloons filled with hot air.

At this time Graham was much dependent on his friends, Pitcur, his brother David, Amerirclose and big rumbustious Dunfermline, to whom he became atached.

Lochiel the Chief of Clan Cameron sent word pledging his men and added the footnote that Keppoch would be back with his force. Dunfermline returned with sixty Gordons, fourteen of them skilled horsemen.

There was that about the Highlanders which never ceased to amaze their Commander. In a day, if pushed to it, they could march forty miles, with no apparent fatigue at the end of it. They were inured to cold, and could go hungry for a length of time, which no lowland soldier could have endured. If the cavalry were put to the canter, with a clansman holding onto each stirrup strap, they would still be there, three miles later, unblown and spoiling for a fight. Later, Lochiel informed Dundee that a clansman could live for a fortnight on a stone of oatmeal and burn- water, with no other sustenance. When it came to crossing a river they were expert, finding the best place to ford, with little difficult. One could not doubt that the call to arms, and its answer, was largely driven by the fear, for most of the Clans, of the re-emergence of the Campbells, rather than by loyalty to King James.

At the art of foraging none could surpass the Chief of the Keppoch MacDonalds, Coll. If meat was needed he could be sent out with a party of his followers, and in an area, which had already been searched for cattle, if any were still there, even if carefully hidden, he would find them. At his own admission Coll would give second best to no man as a cattle lifter, but he would say that, his uncle, MacIain, Chief of Glencoe, was his equal. As time passed Dundee gave him the title of "Colonel of the Cows", and a red coat, to wear, as well. To the Highlanders he was "Colla nam Bo", Coll of the Cattle.

But, as with all Chiefs, Dundee found, on occasion, that Coll was hard to handle, being headstrong and much taken up with Clan feuds. At one stage Dundee had to take the unprecedented step of publicly dressing Coll down for holding the town of Inverness to ransom, with the subsequent, likely consequence of the loss of the support of Keppoch's own Clan. However, Coll, though discomfited, had accepted the reprimand. Perhaps his new coat and his title were more important? Or had the look of disregard from the, grey eyes of his General turned him to stone, as those eyes could so easily do, when they became cold and as merciless as the icicles hanging from the roof of Ossian's cave?

In the first week in May the Commander – in – Chief despatched a letter to every Clan, from whom he thought there was the remotest hope of support, in which he called on them to appear, on the twenty fifth of May, under arms, at the Field of Dalcomera, on the left bank of the River Spean, where it joined the Lochy.

Fretting at the delay Dundee decided that action, in the interval, was needed, for a variety of reasons. In the knowledge that MacKay was a long way off, in camp at Elgin, he was set on a raid south. They went by way of the Pass of Corryaick. As they crossed the summit they were in a wild and lonely country. There was still drift lying in the clutch of the gullies, the land braided and badged with old snow. South west of them the great hills of Nevis reared, Aoanach Mor and the Ben prominent. Beyond the plain of the salmon-stream of Spey reared the Cairngorms, the Blue Mountains, noble and imperious, their heads robed in the white ermine of a recent fall.

It was a new and unfamiliar country to Dundee, but alive with wonder, which lurked everywhere. He knew that he must reverence it and cherish it. But, it had to be savoured for the moment, for, as well he knew, no view ever appeared the same, under the ever-changing sky. Beauty had to be enjoyed, for it was fleeting, fragile and often intangible. At last, down the slope, they came to the farm of Presmuckerach.

Next morning they were off early going south by way of Glen Truim, with mountains on either hand. As they passed the Hills of the Pigs, the Boar of Badenoch and the Sow of Atholl, far off a pair of eagles hung, seeming motionless, majestic, not hunting prey, but watching man.

As they went down by the side of River Garry, which was at its summer level, showing all its spate-tormented rocks, the landscape gradually changed, becoming softer as they lost altitude. Trees became more plentiful, alder and birch and hazel. At Bruar Water they halted for ten minutes to water the horses. From a branch a wren, round as a puff-ball, with its tail cocked up, watched them, its eye a tiny speck of black fire. Three miles further on and they were at Blair Castle, Atholl's seat. His Lordship was from home but they were made exceedingly welcome by his Factor, who was strong for King James's cause. Dundee allowed them only an hour to eat, feed their mounts, and stretch their legs, then they were back in the saddle and off.

By way of the Pass of Killiecrankie they went on, moving ever southwards. Trees now were taller, stronger growing. Land began to appear which was tilled and cropped. At Ballinluig they met the mighty Tay, which there switched its course from flowing easterly to head south.

Nearing Dunkeld, they dismounted, sending three dragoons forward to scout the town, for it was a place, where, because of its strategic position, small detachments of troops were often lodged. Their caution was well founded, for, on their return the scouts reported that there was an officer with six men there, primarily for the collection of taxes.

With no more ado they rode into the town, guided by the scouts, put a ring round the house were the taxmen were staying, ordered them out and put them under arrest. Which, all in all, was unexpectedly fruitful, for they appropriated the tax, "for the King's cause", and were better off by six muskets, seven swords and a pair of pistols, together with powder and shot.

Now the gloaming was coming, the never dark of May, The

evening light kissed the running water of the river and all was soft sibilant sound as it slipped swiftly to the sea. Keen winged swallows and martins hawked insects, in the failing light, skimming the surface, sometimes tipping the ripples with a foot or dipping beaks, effortlessly, to drink at speed. Here, at this cathedral town, the hopes and fears of men seemed far away, immaterial and transient.

For three hours Dundee let his men sleep and the horses be fed and rested, then he had them up and mounted. Off they went, into the night, the light still not gone, pressing ever south. As they went the cloud cover broke and a pale half moon appeared. Already Dundee had issued his orders to his officers, who in turn instructed the troops as they went. At one point owls hung on silver strings, moon touched, hooting in the night. Near the junction of the River Almond with the Tay, as previously arranged, they met up with Thomas Crichton, the Earl of Perth's Chamberlain. To have this man with them was a bonus indeed, for he knew the town of Perth like the back of his hand. For his own part, Dundee was pretty familiar with its streets, having on many occasions ridden down from Dudhope to purchase leather goods or kid-skin gloves for his wife, Perth being the foremost producer, of such, in the kingdom. In ten minutes of talk the Chamberlain had furnished Dundee and his men with all the up to date intelligence of the town. Also he had with him two scaling ladders, each eighteen feet long, which, if plans came to fruition, would prove to be critical for their operation.

Half a mile from the town they dismounted, the bulk of them to wait and rest, whilst Dundee went off, on foot, with twenty of them. Four men carried the ladders. As they approached the ditch along the foot of the defensive wall the stench of it filled their nostrils, foetid and noisome, repulsive in the extreme. No one spoke now, all moving with care. Reaching the ditch Fixer, the best rope man in the Troop, who could tie more knots than anyone else, over lapped the two ladders by some six feet and lashed them together, to form a bridge of thirty feet in length. Then a trooper removed his boots and swam over, his task to see that the end of the ladders did not snag on the farther bank. Swiftly, observing complete silence, everyone crawled across. When all were gathered Fixer cut the ropes and separated the sections of ladders. Both were erected about thirty feet apart, then the men swarmed up and over the wall. Using agreed hand signals Dundee sent his men off, a party to the left and another to the right, to secure the Red Brig Port and the City Port. Swiftly this was accomplished, with the two sentries at each gate being overcome. It took only five minutes to open the Red Brig Port and lower its bridge on its windlass, and a further five minutes for the rest of the force to enter. A flush of excitement and heat welled up in Dundee, running through his body. His scalp tingled and the hairs on his head lifted. He was filled with undiluted adrenaline. Every part of him was alive.

It was two o' clock of the morning. Everyone, apart from those who remained to guard the taken sentries, regrouped at the Skinnergate, then men went off to make sure that the great thirty hundred-weight bell of John the Babtist, which hung in St.John's Kirk, was not allowed to ring out the alarm. Others made for the Spey Tower, where Crichton had reported, troops were billeted. The main group went by way of the Watergate to Gowrie House, where new recruits to a regiment, which the Convention had instructed William Blair of Blair and Lieutenant Robert Pollock to raise, were quartered. Still in silence, the House, built in a U-shape around a courtyard, was secured, no sentries having been posted. Blair and Pollock, who had returned only an hour before, having attended a "Welcome Dinner", put on, in their honour, by the Town Council, were bemused, on being awakened, by a mix of incredulity, fear and the alcohol they had consumed.

In the dead hour before dawn Perth was taken, with no one killed, though there were some sore heads, and without a single citizen having been molested or robbed. Every volunteer had been well warned as to his conduct prior to leaving Dunkeld.

Shyly, in the west the sky turned a marvellous shade of ashes of roses and the clouds were picked out in smoking scarlets with piping of pale gold, as the dawn came up in silent fury. By now they had taken possession of the forty horses which had been collected for the new unit, all of the arms they could find, and the sum of five hundred pounds of taxes, which had been warded in the Tolbooth, all in the King's name.

Rested and fed, burdened with their booty, in a staccato rattle of iron shod hooves, they rode out of the Town, northwards, the Commander on his dark brown stallion, Satan. Surely, this would send a message to the Williamites, let them sweat in Edinburgh. Mackay had looked on Perth as his principal barrier to protect Stirling and the Capital, but, more importantly, a message to the Clan Chiefs? Would the news run through the Glens like molten fire? It was, indeed, a more than hoped for propaganda coup.

With the fervent desire in his heart that the Clans would appear on the twenty fifth, at the Field of Dalcomera, Dundee could spare little time to remain in the south. However, he did allow himself one night with his wife, at his country house in Glen Ogilvie. When they parted, she was full of contrition, at the pass she considered she had brought upon him, by being the daughter of a "rebel", but he would have none of it.

"Jean, I married you for who you are. I married you because I love you. Your family do not enter into it. Let's have an end of it. Soon, I hope, the King will come into his own again and then we can truly be together".

Early morning sunlight flickered on the metal parts of the horses' tack, as if on the scales of a snake, though there was a hint of rain to come. Bridle links rattled. Satan stood, his wide nostrils flared, his fine head up, the eyes taking all in. He had broad, spatulate hooves to cover the soft ground, great lungs in his barrel chest, and the legs and heart to carry his rider hour after hour, an ideal cavalry mount. Without embarrassment Dundee embraced his wife and kissed her full on the mouth, then they parted. She handed her husband a small pouch.

"Go with God, John, this I want you to have, should you need to use it for the King then do so". Her eyes were wet moons, silvered with dripping tears, wondrous, whimsical, hauntingly beautiful. The picture of her face was indelibly etched in the gallery of his mind.

Up into the saddle he swung, his right arm rose, he drove it forwards, , fingers extended, and, never looking back, he led his column off.

Rumour ran round Edinburgh like wildfire at the news from Perth. " Hordes of Highlanders were marching on the Town". "Stirling had already fallen". "King James had come from Ireland

and was at Glasgow". "Those for the Covenant were already being taken and burnt at the stake".

In alarm the Convention ordered more troops into the field.

The name by which the Highlanders knew Dundee," Iain Dubh nan Cath", "Dark John of the Battles", was changed at a stroke by a poem, composed by Iain Lom, the bard, entitled "Iain Gear Dubh nan Cath", "Dark Swift John of the Battles", in which he told of the sixty five mile dash to Perth and of how the Town was taken by Dundee and only twenty men. Faster than the Fiery Cross was ever taken round from clachan to clachan, from bard to bard, the poem passed by word of mouth; in three days there was none in the Highlands who had not heard it.

XXVII. The Ship.

Every year, in mid September, the three masted black ship would ghost into Loch Leven. At its arrival excitement would run through Glencoe, for with it came goods which were unobtainable in Scotland, and the Frenchies brought a panache with them which was quite different from the normal.

Pierre Centille, the Captain, was held in high regard for the way in which he conducted himself, always the gentleman, and, more so, he was the close friend of MacIain.

Almost at once, after anchoring, the Frenchmen would set up booths on the shore, at Invercoe, and put their goods up for trade. Bargaining was hard, but always fair. For their part the Sailors would have lots of things to interest the women, threads and needles, thimbles, lace work, pots of rouge, silken cloth, fine lawn, myriad jewellery, hand mirrors of polished metal, ribbons of every hue, spices, pots, pans, cups and glassware. For the men there were sword blades, which, if you found the right smith, you could have retempered and a hand guard fitted, shoe buckles, whangs, silver buttons, gunpowder smoother and more certain than that to be had from the mills of Edinburgh or Stirling, velvet waistcoats, shirts with elegant lace sleeves, and, most sought after of all, casks of claret, and, if you could afford it, ankers of brandy, a superb drink, smooth beyond belief, like velvet on the pallet, capable of filtering out all of the world's complexities, allowing you to face demons and life itself. There was pig-iron, which the smiths came from far and near to obtain; not as good as the native smelt for making weapons, but it produced a much more malleable iron, ideal for making tools or agricultural implements. And, mother-of –pearl, which the pistol makers, of Stirling and Doune, craved for, for the inlays on the more expensive of the weapons they crafted.

For their part the French took stag-horn, salt herrings, salmon and mackerel by the barrelfull, Cairngorm jem stones, garnets, and amethysts, crafted dirks, cut-silver, goose quills, uisquebaugh, and most prized of all, eider-down, the breast feathers, from the female Dunter Geese, for the stuffing of the bed-quilts of the French Nobles.

Reserved to Mac Iain was the trade in deerhounds. Each year he had three, four or sometimes five for the Captain. Riches indeed, for the French hunters had come to prize them before their own slot-hounds, for their speed of chase and their endless stamina. To own one, in France, for use in the sport of Venary, was to afford one the highest status.

Often MacIain's sons wondered why Centille took the trouble to sail so far? Then they asked him.

"Do you not know why? Has your father never told you?"

"No he has not".

"It is a long story, but it can best be put to you that to him I owe my life, so, each year I come to see my friend, to be beaten by him at Ombre, and to drink with him claret, the secrets of which I taught him. Also, he was the first cattle lifter that I'd ever met who could read and write Latin, Greek, French, English and Gaelic, which he'd learnt to do at the Collegium Scoticum, at the Sorbonne University, in Paris. What better reasons could one ask for?"

"I had gone down to the waterside to pay off the crew on my ship, L'Hirondelle. On the way I stopped at the tavern, "Le Coq Rouge", to have some food and a drink. Unfortunately, my Mate, who always accompanied me on such errands, had injured his leg, the day before, so I was alone. Having eaten I left to go to meet the crew. Their wages were on my person, in a money belt, in coin.

About half a kilometer from the tavern I realised I was being followed. Too late for flight, of a sudden men were all around me. There were five of them, three with cudgels and two with knives".

"Ou est l'argent?" their leader demanded.

"I made no reply. The air was heavy with menace. I felt the first chill of fear. My heart thumped loud in my ears, whilst a coldness stole into my being. One of them lunged at me and swung his club, which I managed to avoid".

"Suddenly, with no warning a giant of a man appeared. He said not a word. Without hesitation he hit one man, with his fist, full in the face. Teeth spilled from his mouth, like pearl-barley strewen from a grain-sower's hand. A knife wielder went for him. As the blade slashed up at him, he shifted his body to avoid the attack, whilst clamping his left hand round the man's wrist in mid-thrust, forcing it downwards. The attacker struggled to bring the knife back up, but the big man slammed the back of his wrist with the outer edge of his palm in a crisp chopping movement. There came the snap of bone, the attacker screamed in pain, then his hand went limp, hanging from his arm at an unnatural angle, the weapon clattering to the ground. In a blur of movement, shatteringly fast, he picked up the dropped cudgel, swung it and hit another foe, who, as a result of the impact flew through the air, his face contacting a wall, the force moulding it to the shape of the stonework; and, as gravity took his body earthwards, great gouges were torn out of his cheek. An attacker went for him, he leant away, bending half over. Then, using every muscle in his back he swung violently upright. From the rear roll to the forward lunge his head described an arc of fifty degrees. His skull weighed, perhaps, about the same as a double round-shot in a medium gun. It bore down until his forehead impacted with the middle of his opponent's face. It was a truly great blow. At sea we call it the "Sailor's Nod", on land it is sometimes referred to as the "Kiss of Scotland". With a crash the last man standing collapsed like an aged oak in a storm. Catching a club-wielder by the scruff of his neck he lifted him and threw him over the wall into the River Sienne. About him was a rhythmic fighting grace, which could only have been born of experience. At that, the scrap was over, one man running off. Blood was seeping through the big man's right sleeve, he must have been stabbed in the arm".

"Are you alright, let's see your wound?" I enquired.

"His lips curled back, then he informed me that it only pained a little and it was minor, nothing like as bad as he'd had before. So, I took him back to the tavern, where the Landlord's wife dressed the cut. There were old white wound marks on the knuckles of his sword hand and on his forearm a cross- hatch of healed scars, which glistened like a pale web. All there knew that they were in the presence of a warrior. The Landlord's wife was amazed at the patient's size, not only his height, but that he had the body bulk to compliment it".

"I asked him where he had come from, and why he had come to my aid?"

"Many times I have sat in change houses, all over the Highlands of Scotland, after drovers have sold their cattle, at a sale and I have seen men leave, to go after them, to relieve them of their money. All of the signs were there. Men with eyes that were never still, shallow stone-cold eyes; men who had an abundance of guile in their eyes, men who were furtive, men awaiting a sign to go, from their leader, who often had the eyes of a stoat, with all of its attributes before it descends into a rabbit warren to begin slaying. Besides I did not consider that the odds of five to one were very fair."

"So that is how our friendship began".

In the two and a half years MacIain spent at the university, in Paris, the friendship between himself and Centille blossomed. Pierre's family owned a fleet of six ships, with Pierre's as Captain of L'Hirondelle. Over the last hundred years or so the family had built up a trading business, in the main, built on wine, which they delivered to England, the Low Countries, Scandinavia and ports around the Mediterranean, with occasional trips to North Africa, though the Moorish pirates were troublesome.

Often the two men played Boule, to which Pierre had introduced MacIain. There was a satisfaction on throwing the heavy balls to where you wanted them to rest, and often a greater satisfaction in pitching a ball, just right, so that it knocked your opponents ball out of a winning position. Other evenings they spent in drinking wine and eating Brie cheese, of which the Scotsman had become very fond.

On four occasions, when the University was closed for holidays, the Captain took MacIain on a voyage with him and deepened his knowledge of wine and brandy, by so doing. First, they sailed into the mighty River Gironde, which split into a swallow-tail, the northern branch becoming the Dordogne and the southern the Garone. They took the southern route and arrived at the ancient town of Bordeaux, with its great churches, which were visited by people on the pilgrim road to Santiago de Compostela. Around Saint-Michel, with its narrow, twisting streets Mac Iain was enchanted by the character and the ever-changing aspects of the place.

Whilst the ship was being loaded with cargo Pierre took the Highlander off to further his knowledge of the wines of the area. He explained, in between tastings, that on the Graves peninsula, you could find two of the Bordeaux's great clarets, the Medocs and the Graves, nurtured and cultivated on the narrow strip of land stretching from the city to the mouth of the river, drained by dozens of little streams. In the Medoc the soil was very high in iron content, which, coupled with the long, hot humid summers, afforded the grapes plenty of time to ripen and be harvested. Pierre showed how the wines of Graves were fuller and coarser than the Medocs, and had an unusually long life. Twenty miles east of Bordeaux, beyond the Dordonge River was the place of the third, the strong, dark reds, robust, virile and intense, the St. Emilion. MacIain could only agree, for was not the proof of the taste of the wine the drinking of it? In five days he had never drunk so continually. Each night, at whatever inn they lodged at, after eating, both of them were ready only for sleep.

With the ship now having its allotted cargo they sailed north for La Rochelle, there to fill the one remaining empty hold with brandy. There would be no problem with the twice distilled spirit, for it could travel anywhere. It came from two grapes, grown on chalky soil. With care it was, like whisky, distilled in copper pot-stills and then casked in oak for from five to fifty years, after which up to half of the contents would have disappeared, lost through the wood, to become "The Portion of the Angels".

"One should look for a genuinely dark golden colour for a sign of proper age and quality", instructed Pierre.

In the old part of the town Pierre's father had an apartment, where he lived, in semi-retirement. That he was a character Mac Iain found out, at there first meeting. He was charismatic and magnetic, with a bold stare under hooded eyes, with huge tangled eyebrows, handsome in a dark saturnine way. Both men instantly took a liking to each other. After a welcoming drink of the very best brandy they talked on a wide range of subjects, until they found that they both had a mutual love of hunting deer.

"Next time, when you are to come again, get Pierre to forewarn me, and we will hunt together". And, so they did.

Hunting deer in France, MacIain found, was very different from hunting in Scotland. In France the deer were much bigger, up to a third heavier, and they were woodland beasts, not the red deer of the high tops. They were slower and not as swift, though they had learnt different tricks; how to lose themselves in a thicket, or to lie down in long grass so that they could not be seen. There range of colour was not as varied as the Highland deer, though, in woodland their camouflage was superb. If they remained motionless it was almost impossible to pick them out. However, it was the observance of the ceremony of the hunting, which MacIain was intrigued with. Everything was formalised. Everyone engaged in the hunt was dressed, accordingly, in a uniform, to denote his function. Each individual had a very specific part to play. Also, there were dogs, countless dogs, there were slot-hounds specially trained to follow the hoof-prints of the animals, sleuth-hounds to follow scent, and the large sight-hounds, which were slipped when a stag was in full view, to bring it to bay. Ceremonies or old traditional rites were observed at virtually each stage of the hunt, before, during and after, whether it be to honour the dogs, the men or the deer. MacIain found it all very strange, but undeniably exciting.

Pierre's father found it hard to believe that the Clansmen only used one type of dog, the deer-hound, which did everything needed, except to put their noses to the ground, so that, as a result they were never trained as trackers. MacIain explained that the deer-hounds were so high-couraged that often they would not bay the stag, but would pull him down or be antler pierced or killed, by him, before the huntsman came up.

Of the deer-hounds Old Centille wanted to hear more, so the Chief told him of the dogs of Glencoe, of how they were a hand or sometimes a hand and a half taller than the hounds from anywhere else in the Highlands, as a consequence of which they were stronger and swifter and more powerful.

"There must be a reason for them being larger?"

"There is indeed".

So Mac Iain told him of how, fifteen hundred years ago, King

Erragon of Sora had come into Loch Leven, with forty snake ships, full of men, and tried to overcome the men of Glencoe. They had fought for five days, with no side achieving victory. With them, the invaders had brought huge war-dogs, a third to half as heavy again than a deer-hound. Many hounds had been slain and men also by their sheer power, but the hounds had been quick to learn, they took to working in pairs, running in with their superior speed, one on each side of the large dogs, gripping them by the ears, until one could, whiplash fast, take a throat hold. During the fifth night, Fingal, The Chief, had had a trench dug on the slope of The Pap of Glencoe, in which he secreted thirty of his best spearsmen. When dawn came on the sixth day the Glencoe men retreated to the base of the hill and then started to withdraw up the face, with the men of Sora in pursuit. At, what he deemed to be the correct moment, Fingal had led the spearmen in the "going down", which had proved to be decisive. Almost at once the foe broke and was routed. Great had been the slaughter, with the ever diminishing number of survivors being driven eastwards towards Kinlochleven. At the narrows of the loch the remnants of the enemy stopped to make a stand. There the deer-hounds, which had outrun their masters, had attacked and had either slain or had caused to drown in the shallows, nearly all of the remaining warriors. From that day to this, for fifteen centuries, the narrows has been named, Caloasnacoan, The Tide-race of the Dogs, to honour the deer-hounds. Of the forty snake ships, which had come, there was only enough crew to enable two to sail away. And in the course of time, the few war dogs, which still lived, had mated with the Glencoe deer-hounds and given them, generation after generation, the gene, which ensured that their offspring were larger.

"Fantastique, that is truly a marvellous story. Now, I have the hope that I will see these mervilleuse dogs".

"And so you shall", said Mac Iain, "for I will send one to you when I return home".

Thus was born the trade in deer-hounds, between Glencoe and the Centilles. Eventually, the deer hunters of France all wanted to possess a Highland hound, in particular one that had also been fully trained before leaving the Glen.

XXVIII. TO KILLIECRANKIE

Great was the welcome they had from Lochiel, when they returned. At once the Chief provided a house for Dundee, on the banks of the River Roy. Haliburton of Pitcur, a friend of long standing lodged with him. It was good to be with Sir Ewan Cameron of Lochiel again, the old warrior, who had fought many a good fight, and to have Dunfermline, Dunkeld, his brother David, and James Philip of Almericlose, whom he had made his Standard Bearer, with him; all loyal beyond reproach. His great regret was that Balcarres still languished in prison.

A great comfort to Dundee was his Troop, composed of the men who had followed him from England. They would fight for him before any other. To them he personified their soul. He was their cause. He held them together as no other could, and they knew it. As cavalry, they could not be equalled.

On the field of Dalcomera gorse bushes blazed golden in the sunlight. From early morning men had come in. There was, as the day drew on, a growing volume of sound, talk, the clink of arms, pipes at play. Gradually the numbers present increased. For his part Dundee was content. Three days before written confirmation, from King James's own hand, had arrived, appointing him as Commander – in – Chief of James's forces. Also Colonel Canon had arrived, from Ireland, with three hundred men and thirty five barrels of gunpowder, match, ball and flints. And now the coming in of the Clans was providing him with the means to take on MacKay. Much of his time was spent in meeting the Chiefs as they arrived, some known and others never met before. Lochiel attended him and made the introductions. Most of the Chiefs were very young, though all were fierce for war. They radiated a palpable pride. They were all avid to fight. Men bred to bear arms and to fight in inter-clan forays. Tradition had prepared them to be formidable soldiers. Certainly Lochiel and MacIain of Glencoe stood out as being most senior in years. Of all the men present MacIain was outstanding for his size. He stood nineteen and three quarter hands high, with the body bulk to match, a truly formidable figure. Long moustached, dressed in a buff coat, with a brass bell-mouthed blunderbuss on his back and a huge broad sword at his side. His the graceful walk and the hard warrior air about him. When he bowed it was very slightly and stiffly, as if admitting to no superior rank."Give me ten of them", thought Dundee, "And I'll need no more". The certainty of victory grew within him. He felt the cloak of it settle on his shoulders.

His intelligence was nearly always better than the information had by the Government forces. MacKay was reported to still be in Edinburgh, but of the opinion that Atholl was no longer a safe territory, he was strongly minded to take Blair Castle, which would give him control of the hill passes to the north. In turn Dundee knew that Blair was of the greatest strategic importance, also, most important of all, he knew that the Clans would not hold together long without action. Therefore, he decided to move for it, at once. Though, not without opposition. Other reinforcements were still to come in, and there were those who thought they should wait until they arrived. In particular, Colonel Canon was so minded. Nevertheless, the Commander-in-Chief took the decision to march south, despite knowing that MacKay's forces outnumbered his by at least two to one. Alasdair Dubh MacDonnell said that the Highlanders were like no other troops, that they were hardier and above all they wanted to engage the enemy. This opinion Lochiel concurred with, and, any doubt Dundee had, was swept away. "All the world be with us, blessed be God".

At midnight they were at Blair, where, once again Baleichin, the factor, made them welcome. There was no sign of any enemy and no one had heard anything of them.

XXIX. THE ONSET.

Above all the King needed a victory, Dundee knew this and was set on it. Having Blair Castle to his rear, held for him, this, allied to the Clansmens' stated desire to engage the enemy at once, stiffened his resolve. Excitement rose in him and, with no conscious thought, he became drunk with the leading of an army. He had intelligence of MacKay being at Dunkeld with some four thousand troops. To engage James's forces MacKay would have to come by way of the defile of the Pass of Killiecrankie. He realised that by taking his men into the Pass he would be unable to give battle. On the other hand, if he permitted the enemy to come through, they could engage on ground to the north- west. Victory would, in his considered opinion, be best achieved by use of the Highland charge, which was always at its most effectual, when made downhill to achieve maximum impetus. In which case, he determined to take the high ground. Avoiding the easiest route of advance by the Old Road from Blair; he despatched a small troop of Horse to divert MacKay's attention. Marching up Glen Fender, after crossing the River Tilt, the Clans skirted the northern edge of Lude Hill and descended by way of the burn of Allt Chuluain, moving forward, south- eastward, along a ridge, to the lower slopes of Creag Fallaich. They were now some three hundred feet above the foe.

Soft the wind came out of the west, with little air moving. The woods were musical with the song of birds. Trailing strings of gulls hung far off, distant above the river. Nearer still, lapwings flung themselves against the clouds, uttering lonely cries. Water chuckled over stones, sifting shillet, or ran in a rush, in the narrows, between the rocks; never still, even in the depths of inky pools, its murmur ever present.

With practised skill the Williamite army took up position facing westwards towards Strathgarry, with its left flank anchored on the river and its right extended along a ridge beside the Allt Chuluain. However, on observing the Clans arraying themselves on ground other than that expected, MacKay, experienced General that he was, became immediately aware of the danger to his disposition, which caused him to reform his troops to the right and make them march up the hill, by which means he took ground suitable for defence, but not for attack. Now their backs were to the precipitous defile of the River Garry. In order to prevent being outflanked, especially towards the Pass, MacKay extended his line until they were only three deep, with no reserves and separated, in places, by tracts of bog. Nevertheless, he was well aware that he outnumbered the enemy by more than two to one.

With satisfaction, Dundee observed that things were moving as he had hoped they would. He packed his men into tight regiments, each composed of a major clan or its septs and adherents. With him he had the greatest gathering, for battle, of the Clan Donald, since they had gone down the hill, with his relative, the great Montrose, thirty years before, at Inverlochy, and dunged the ground with the bodies of fifteen hundred of the Clan Campbell. The MacLeans, two hundred strong, he placed on the right flank, with next to them his three hundred Irish under Colonel Pearson, then Clanranald with six hundred and Glengarry with his three hundred. In the centre he stanced his forty five Horse, with two hundred Cameron men to the left, directly opposed to MacKay's own Regiment. Anchoring his left Dundee had three hundred MacDonalds of Sleat and more MacLeans.

To his left MacKay had two thousand two hundred and fifty battle hardened veterans; troops who had fought, in fight after fight, on continental Europe. On his right he had two thousand three hundred, who were mainly unblooded Lowland Scots or English recruits.

Lachlan felt the fear building within him. He had been on many a creich, had often known danger, but it had never been like this. Now, it had come to the arbitrement of war, the sword and bullet would decide; battle was about to be joined; men would die; there would be courage and there would be cowardice. Most of all, the lad feared that he would not acquit himself well, that he would disgrace the Clan. Thoughts of Elspeth flooded into his mind, would he ever see her again? The picture of her face rose before his eyes, the gold of her hair, soft as blown thistle down, her eyes the colour of August cornflowers. He looked around, MacIain stood erect, his tall powerful bulk put him head and shoulders above any man there. The breeze stirred his long moustaches, the seasoned campaigner. On his back was slung his gun, which had become his hallmark, a brass bell mouthed blunderbuss, which he'd acquired whilst on a cattle lifting raid deep into Strathspey. It was seldom that he did not have it about his person. At his side hung his huge broadsword, Swan's Wing, one third longer than that carried by a man of normal stature. Iain, MacIain's elder son, the Chif Designate, was there, Tearlach Og, and to his left, in the most garish of multi-hued tartans was MacNeill of Barra.

Dundee, accompanied by Cameron of Lochiel, rode up and down the line on his dark stallion, dismounting frequently to talk to a Chief or a man he recognised, mostly in English, but sometimes in the halting Gaelic phrases which they'd come to know from him. There was a glory about him, which is given to few; he owned a personal magic, which bound men to him, particularly warriors. Most of all, they loved him because he was not a man of peace, but, because he was a man of war. They knew that in him they had a leader, for whom, perhaps, battle was the ultimate experience, the reason for being.

A hawk flew over casting its fast moving sickle winged, transient, shadow on the grass as it passed. Behind, stood Carn Liath, a hill of smouldering grey. From right to left the tartans embroidered the slope with a moving curtain of colour; the red of Keppoch, the blue, red and green of Clanranald, the rich red of the MacAllisters, the green and blue of Glengarry and the sett of Sleat, red with green bars. On their bonnets the Clan MacDonald wore ling, the MacLeans blackberry heath, the Camerons a sprig of oak.

MacKay's troops were armed with Brown Bess muskets and short swords. They wore long full-skirted red coats, grey breeches and blue Highland Bonnets. Sergeants wore white spatter-dash gaiters.

Behind the Horse, James Philip, Dundee's Standard Bearer, had set up the flag, which hung limply against its staff in the still air. From below came the tuck of drums beating out an age-old army tattoo. At once the great war- pipes began to answer. Lachlan, instantly, felt thrilled. "Gilliechrist", the war tune of Glengarry, sounded out, fierce and proud..

At Locheil's command all of the pipes fell silent. Then, on his next order, the Clansmen lifted their voices in a fell chorus, the cries harsh, almost wolflike in their tone, they pulsed and throbbed, as if they had been tapped into an atavistic, irrational savagery. It had the timbre of sheer joy at the battle to come. MacKay's troops, particularly the raw recruits, heard the cries and many shivered, for to them, it seemed as if the veneer of civilisation had been stripped away exposing the dark side of humanity, the cruel, the irrational, the animal instinct of alien ancestors, terrifying the innermost recesses of their psyche. Suddenly, they would cease their clamour and once more down the brae would come the jaunting notes of the bagpipes. All of the rest of the afternoon Dundee gave over to the unnerving of his opponents, alternately interspersing the pipe music with cheers and jeers, which rolled down the slope in waves of malevolent sound.

With total aplomb MacKay strode about talking to his officers. He was a master of war, blooded and hardened by countless battles against some of the finest armies on Continental Europe. Where anyone stood, or on what ground they chose, he did not give a fig for, for he would beat them anyway, and, at the head of his troops, he would march forward, triumphant, to take Blair Castle. "Who should be afraid of those bundles of rags arrayed above us?" That was his message.

Dundee kept his clansmen leashed and would not slip them, though at times they were sorely provoked by MacKay's men, who frequently tried to draw them by firing muskets into their ranks, and on occasion loosening off one of their ineffectual light cannon.

Many of the Clan Chiefs renewed old acquaintanceships. Glengarry, MacIain, Ardshiel and young Stewart of Appin, who were all old friends, engaged in banter and swapped anecdotes. At the head of his men of Keppoch, Colla nam Bo, Coll of the Cows, stood out, resplendent in his Colonel's red coat, which Dundee had given him the month before, when he had promoted him. It was rumoured that he'd never taken it off his back since, and that he even slept in it.

"I would be counting it a privilege if my men could stand with yours?" an auburn- headed man enquired of MacIain.

"They can indeed, for, when we go down the brae, what better men to have beside one than those of Rob Roy MacGregor and his father, the Colonel Donald?"

MacIain had never been, before, in a fight with Rob Roy, a relation by marriage, who, already, at nineteen years of age, had a fearsome reputation as a swordsman. His inordinately long arms, which gave him advantage in the use of his weapon, hung down at his sides. It was averred that he could tie his garters without having to stoop, and some said he could lace his brogans similarly. He was a commanding man, not because of his reputation, but because of his presence, which seemed to flare like flame, for everything about him was red, the hair on his head, his great bush of a beard, and the vibrant red MacGregor tartan which he wore.

Amongst the Redcoats the raw recruits were haunted by the sounds of the pipes, for many of them had never heard them before. The afternoon passed, like drips of water, falling one on one, into the well of time. Rumour had it that this foe, now arrayed before them, was bloody, barbarous and inhuman. But, most of all, the eerie, discordant, keening put the fear of death into them. Nerves ate at their stomachs. Tension slowly rose. As the day drew on into evening the Williamite army became gradually more silent. No one in the lines spoke much, dread had built in them with the long period of inactivity.

Many of the Highlanders began to become restive thinking that if Dundee did not let them go, soon, it would be too dark to see the foe.

"Are you still afeart lad?" MacIain asked Lachlan. "Have a pull at that then". He handed the boy a silver flask with its top unscrewed.

Lachlan drank deeply and at once began to cough, the rich French Cognac burning at his throat. Later, much later, when he was to think back, he was to know the value of that drink.

They knew it would be soon, for Dundee had walked along the line, stopping to talk to each Chief in turn, conversing with them and asking for their views. He showed no surprise, but felt much when the Old Fox of Glencoe, MacIain, gave him some lines from Homer's Iliad -----

> "Ah, could we but survive this war
> To live forever deathless, without age,
> I would not ever go again to battle,
> Nor would I send you there for honour's sake!
> But now a thousand shapes of death surround us,
> And no man can escape them, or be safe.
> Let us attack – whether to give some fellow
> glory or to win it from him."

Whereupon Dundee, perhaps inspired, had given his army the Brosnach, the Gaelic incitement to battle, calling upon the ancient MacDonald exhortation, given by MacMhuirich, two hundred and fifty years before, at the Battle of Red Harlaw, "Remember, you Sons of Conn, hardihood in time of strife". Also, he had passed on, through Lochiel, the Cameron spur, "Come Sons of the Dog go let us eat flesh". He had spoken of the King, and of Country, and given them his slogan for the battle, *King James and the Church of Scotland*.

It was as beautiful a summer's evening as God had ever given as a blessing on a wicked world. As the light softened it washed the land in gold. All around the hills stood in pride, aureate touched. Imperceptibly the gold seeped away, soft shadows were gathering in the hollows. As the sun sank very slowly below the horizon a pool of deep carmine spilled across, then, the redness paled and threw its diluted fire on the mass of the hills, and, farther off the mountains were wrapped in purple. Now the sun was no longer in the Clansmens' eyes.

The pipes fell silent, as did James's army. All eyes were on Dundee, who sat his horse, out before the mass of the troops, his sword raised.

MacArthur, the supreme piper there, strode forward and blew up, on his great war- pipe, "The Flames of Wrath".

Light flashed, cruel and beautiful, from Dundee's sword, as he slashed it down to signal the onset. With a great shout his army were at the "a dol sios", the "going down", many discarding their plaids and any other encumbrances on the way.

XXX. THE CHARGE.

They went down the slope, their war cries full throated, ululating in bursts of sound, totally committed and utterly fierce; for them only death would slake their thirst for the life blood of their foes. As they ran the ground thrummed to the pounding of their feet, so that it trembled like a drumhead.

Sergeants, in the age- old- fashion of battle, yelled at their men to keep their lines straight, as the Clans came at them. The air was filled with the rank smell of fear-sweat, an odour, known to fighting men, since time began. As a result of the dispositions the Macleans, on the right wing, had some two hundred yards further to run, which meant that they received an extra volley. There was a momentary slowing of their impetus as shot men went down, but still they drove on. Not for nothing were the known as the "Sliochd a' Chaidhleimh Iaruinn", "The Race of the Iron Sword". If a man fell or died, be he friend or foe, they stepped over his corpse as if it was a stone, for there was neither time nor breath for anything more. They jinked over the dead and dying, pouring on in a tartan flood. Feathers of gun smoke spurted into the air, misting the land. Two men ran past Lachlan; when the light touched their hair it flared like fire in tall grass. At once he knew them for Rob Roy and his father Donald. Above the yelling and the bang of guns the sound of the pipes cut through, the music of war, stern and fierce. Now his fear had left him, adrenaline pumped through him, and he felt the wild exhilaration of battle lust. All was a blur of merging colours and dynamic movement.

At thirty yards the Highlanders fired their matchlocks, as Dundee had instructed, in one single volley, which crashed, hugely loud, in the evening air, as every gun spoke almost as one; the salvo sounding like the bellow of rolling thunder. Iain heard the distinctive dunt of is father's blunderbuss as it loosed off hurling two handfuls of goose shot from its bell shaped muzzle. The guns were flung down. Swords, the aristocrats of weapons, sung from their scabbards.

Frantically, the red coated riflemen attempted to fix bayonets, or the veterans tap loaded their guns, to increase their speed of fire, not bothering to use their ram rods, slamming their musket butts hard on the ground, trusting that the blow would jar the ball down to the loose powder charge below. Mouths were sour with the sodden taste of gunpowder. Flaming scraps spat from the musket locks as they were fired. Lead balls thudded in, through the tartan, to cause excruciating pain or to kill..

With an easy grace for such a large man, Lachlan saw MacIain, big boned and strong, back swing his sword and a redcoat reeled away spilling blood. Another man tried to spear the Chief with his bayoneted Brown Bess musket, but he side stepped and drove the point of his broadsword into his chest; the soldier arched his spine and screamed, a high animal sound, which was, almost instantaneously, cut off as air hissed out of his lungs, then his blood spewed forth, bright and keen, in a relentless stream. Of a sudden, Lachlan was faced with a foeman who ran at him armed with a short sword. Instinctively, he lunged and there was an instant's resistance, then the point entered the skin and muscles to tear into the blood vessels of the neck. There was a great scream of fear, which fell to silence, as the man died. Bright as a cut garnet, a gobbet of blood splashed from his lips. As he fell the weight of his body ripped it clear of the blade.

In the centre, Dundee, with his Horse, charged MacKay's cavalry, who did not wait to receive them but wheeled about and fled for the Pass.

Men came down in groups of ten to fifteen, often a whole related family or a bunch of close friends; the speed of their approach and the easy grace of their run over rough ground or through bog, was awe inspiring. Even the Dutch Brigade, veterans of countless Continental battles, had never encountered such a swift engagement.

There was a great cry of "Fraoch Eilean", the MacDonald battle slogan, and calls of "King James"; the air was filled with a sound like the barking of dogs, wild for the scent of blood, then the full weight of the charge struck. Weapons flashed in the fading light like the transient touch of moonlight on water. There was noise all around, shouting and the clash of steel, sword rasped on sword. Blades slashed into necks and laid open ribs. There was the occasional flash of a Williamite musket. A knot of redcoats had gathered round their battalion colours, sergeants with long handled axes, officers with swords and men with bayonets. Purcell's Irish drove in on them. A Major of Ramsay's ran at them; a blade took him in the belly; he screamed and his sword dropped. All around was disorder, men fought, a pace apart. Screams rent the air, wild, agonising sounds, tearing at the heart, rending eardrums.

Fastest of all was the left wing, composed mainly of MacDonalds and Camerons, but bolstered by the Macleans of Otter and the MacNeils of Barra; it struck MacKay's Regiment, who stood in platoon order, and fired three withering volleys, but, the line, only three deep, could not resist the weight of the charge. With a clash, and the shock of body against body, and the clang of swords, they met. There were short violent minutes of strife, then, from terror stricken pockets, within the formation, panic flared like a gale driven fire. Suddenly, the red line broke; then began the slaughter. It was chaos now, with those in retreat being hunted down. They ran for safety, but few escaped. Most were skewered on the broad swords.

On the right wing Glengarry ran straight down on Kenmure's. Many fell, shot; Glengarry's brother among them. Suddenly the firing all but ceased, apart from some sporadic bullets loosed off. It became strangely quiet. The great war- pipes blew and the sound overbore all. Kenmure's troops were struck by the flight of their own cavalry, which brought such instant disorder that they broke and ran. MacKay, noting that his cavalry was in disarray, called on the horsed officers to follow him. He spurred forward, with little regard for his own safety. Almost at once, he was amongst the muskets' smoke, which hung, close to the ground, in a blue grey mist. Not drawing rein he plunged on to break out into clear air, where upon he realised that he had become isolated and detached from his comrades.

Balfour's regiment, who, a moment before, had been rigid in their formal line, struck by the Macleans clansmen, buckled and broke. It was chaos now, with those in retreat being hunted. It was a wild killing, totally abandoned and untrammelled, swords whistled their death song as they cleaved the air. Men running were almost certain to be cut down, yet fear drove them, with the thought, ---------- the single thought, ---------   that, of escape. With a bravery born of an amalgam of hopelessness and the arrogance, which is given to some, when death stares them in the face, Lieutenant Colonel Mackay, the General's brother, with his coterie of officers, stood his ground, fought and was slain.

Such was the thrust of the Cameron men that they went straight through the lines and missed Leven's regiment. As they passed it they were fired upon and suffered huge losses. Lochiel had gone too far left, and, as a result, they swept through the now fleeing ranks of MacKay's, striking only the left- hand edge of Hasting's infantry, the Thirteenth Regiment of Foot.

Sudden and savage elation flared in Dundee like the bite of raw spirit. In a single swift sweep of the view of the field he saw that victory was his for the taking. He felt the mantle of it settle on his shoulders. The Government forces were in disarray, their lines shattered. Those of the enemy, who could, were streaming away, routed, in full flight. Everything he and his Highlanders had striven for, for the King, had come to pass. He marvelled that, even in the press of battle one could find joy; it sang through his being.

In the centre smoke hung in a dense mist obscuring much of the action. Some of Hasting's were still firing as Dundee, on his dark horse, spurred out of the enveloping cloud; seeing him go Pitcur and Dumfermline galloped after him. At once Dundee noted that his left did not fare as well as his forces did on his right. He turned and rose in the saddle, lifting his arm to beckon Wallace's men to come up with him, whereupon, a musket ball took him in the side, a hand's breadth below his breast plate, bringing him from the saddle. Smoke billowed and surged in a blue fog. At full speed Dumfermline and Pitcur with fourteen other troopers thundered after the Williamite cavalry in its mad dash for the Pass.

One battalion, Leven's stood, almost intact, while on the right, with great composure, Colonel Fernando Hastings had wheeled his men to let the MacDonalds through. One half of his battalion was still in place. On their return, Dunfermline and his companions, after pursuing the enemy horse, were amazed to find some of their foes still drawn up in ranks. Without hesitation Dumfermline, assisted by Lochiel's son-in-law, who had the gaelic, gathered about sixty men and mounted an attack on Hasting's, but Leven's advanced to engage them and they were forced to disperse, seeing that they would be overrun. As Dumfermline retreated he came upon Dundee lying on the ground, tended by a soldier, named Johnston, who had caught him as he fell from his horse. Just then Leven's muskets opened fire and Dunfermline's mount was shot under him. Pitcur took a ball, from which he was to die two days later. Gilbert Ramsay the soldier-lawyer was killed, shot through the heart. Heedless of danger, amidst the bullets, Dumfermline ran back to where Dundee lay. At once he saw that his friend was not yet dead, but in his eyes was the shadow, which told that his shade was called. With gentleness Johnston cradled his head and with his free hand wiped his lips with a wet cloth.

"How fares the fight?" asked Dundee.

"The day goes well for the King, but I am sorry for what has befallen your Lordship".

As the life ebbed from him Dundee whispered his last words, "It matters less for me, seeing that the day goes well for my Master". He tried vainly to speak further but the words were drowned; for a moment the farewell was there, in his eyes, then the pupils dilated, the irises went, their grey driven away, to be taken over by a featureless transparent black. His body jerked, once, twice, thrice, and it was over, he was dead. Grief and shock was all that Dumfermline felt as he looked into the lucent, vacant windows of the grey eyes he'd come to know so well. With infinite tenderness he reached out and closed them for the last time.

Meanwhile, Mackay, realising, soldier that he was, his forces, being in retreat, his duty was to bring them off the field, in good order, to save as many of them as he could. To this end, in the deepening twilight, he gathered Leven's together and marched them to join Hasting's, some four hundred in all. The men of Clan Menzies, in their distinctive red and white tartan, who had fought alongside Leven, had already informed him of the Ford of Raineach, which crossed the Garry to the west of the Chine Burn. With care he placed the remnant of Colonel Lawder's Fusiliers along the lip of the defile which led steeply down to the ford, where, even there, the water surged and roared in spate, after three nights of heavy rain. These Fusiliers, all two hundred of them he had looked upon as the cream of his army, now only thirty remained.

"Sergeant Major can you hold the Clans whilst our troops cross the river?"

"Sir, it will be the Fusiliers pleasure".

"Then I wish you good shooting and commend you and your men for their gallantry".

With that Mackay wheeled his horse and went down the steep slope, through the long ferns, to oversee the crossing of the river, which ran in flood, dark, peat stained, splashing over great boulders on its long run down to the sea. With weapons at the high port, in an attempt to keep them dry, the men waded over, breast deep, the strong flow ballooning out their coats. Some, having paid no heed to the advice of the Menzies men to always face up stream and to sidle across holding on to a fellow soldier, or perhaps weakened by wounds, or due to clumsiness, stumbled and were swept away to drown. However, MacKay would, in time, look back, and realise that this operation had been the most successful part of his otherwise disastrous day. In the deepening gloom they marched off, guided by the Menzies; perhaps, wisely going south, towards Strathtay, rather than by way of the Pass, where the Highlanders were killing all of the enemy they could find.

As long as the light held men died. The slaughter went on in a savage orgy of battle lust, until merciful darkness forced it to halt. Night covered the world with its wings.

As it lit, high in the sky, the Blood Star burned, like a wound, in the flesh of the Sky God.

XXXI. AFTER BATTLE.

In the night many of the wounded had succumbed to their injuries or had died at the hands of the gleaners, who never failed to arrive on site after any battle. Where they came from, or who they were, could never be established with any certainty, but, always, without fail, these ghouls materialised, never to be seen, for they were people of the darkness, who could work without lights and in total silence. In a few moments they could strip a corpse of every item of clothing, missing not a single trophy or prize, be it a locket or a few coins sewn into the hem of a coat, a knife, or any other weapon, food, or a water bottle. If necessary, in total silence, they could, with infinite skill, cut a still-living victim's throat, should they deem it expedient.

MacIain was sorely troubled, for, ever since the fight, there had been no trace of Iain. Inverigan and Lachlan had reported that they had seen him go downhill about five or six paces to the left of his father, in the charge, but none of the Clan had seen anything of him thereafter. He did not show it, for, as Chief, he had to carry the greater responsibility of the well being of the Clan; he felt bereft, as if no fire on earth could thaw the despair, which had settled in an icy ring round his heart. What would he say to Mary? She had pleaded with him not to take Iain, to support Dundee, but he had overridden her request, knowing that the Clan warriors would expect Iain, as future Chief, to go, and that it was his son's time to add to his experience of war. If he had been killed MacIain hoped that he had made a good death, the death of a warrior, taken in battle. At once a search had been organised for him and for all of the clansmen who were missing. At the muster, after the fight, nineteen, out of the one hundred and two, who had first gone down the hill, were not present. On through the night they had searched, hampered by darkness and the very considerable numbers of dead and dying. By dawn, of the Glencoe men, they had found seven dead and eight wounded, but of Iain there was no sign.

It was almost beyond belief, the carnage. The Enemy lay in the lines in which they had been drawn up, the windrows of the dead. Even the old battle hardened warriors were amazed. Men lay, some with the tops of there skulls cloven off, others cut down from their brain- pan to their breast- bone. Two great pits had been dug, one for the Clansmen, the other for the Redcoats. Five Glencoe men had been posted, by the grave, for the Highlanders, with strict instructions to examine every body, to see if they could come upon Iain. Sergeants had been given the task of collecting arms and equipment, of which there was a considerable haul. In particular, the Government issue Brown Bess muskets would be highly prized by any Highlander, fortunate enough to, eventually, be allotted one.

On the edge of the killing field the ravens and hoodie crows had come down, to sidle forward, to begin to feed on the dead. Why, MacIain wondered, when a stag was slain and the gralloch of the entrails was given to the ravens, as their share, was that accepted without thought, but, when they wanted to take human carrion the flesh cringed?

With tenderness they had wrapped Dundee's body in two plaids and borne him west to Blair, there to lie on the nearest consecrated ground. It had been decided that his funeral should take place a day later, to allow the other dead to be buried and to permit those of the living, who so wished, to attend.

Pipers were in evidence, the air filled with the sound as they blew up for those committed to the earth. All about was the rancid, all pervading smell of death. The ground was scabbed with blood, which had coagulated and hardened. When the dead of Glencoe had been laid to rest and covered with the earth of The Red Field, and had been blessed by a priest, MacEunrig struck up the lament "Winter on the Three Sisters of Shadow". As the pipes crooned the notes went out, to hang, resonant on the air, with a sadness, like beaten drums, but, a sadness which only the pipes can give, to die away in slow, soulful, cadences, in a threnody of grief.

They did not forget to search along the river, for many, in

particular, those of the enemy, had been drowned. In the hour of victory few had been given quarter. At one pool they came upon a circle of bodies, with legs and arms entwined, bobbing on the surface of the water, turning slowly, in a ring, enemies on the field of battle, but comrades in the truce of death. Men jettisoned like flotsam on the open sea. Nine wore red coats and one the tartan of Glencoe. He floated face down, a tall man of over six feet, as was Iain. His long hair drifted as weed would under water. When they had fished him out and turned him over, they found it was not the Chief's son, but the missing Tearlach Og.

Perhaps the spate water had taken Iain's body away, to wash it down past the town of Perth, and eventually, to send it out into the vastness of the Northern Ocean? All knew that it would be better to come upon him dead rather than to never find him, so that they could grieve for him and send him on to his final rest in a fitting manner.

XXXII. THE FUNERAL.

In the night they had taken Dundee, wrapped in two plaids, to Blair Castle.

They had washed and laid out his body and put it in a rowan wood coffin. When they stripped him of his armour they found, hanging from a chord, round his neck, a pouch, in which there were the jewels of his wife, which she had pressed upon him, "for the King", all four hundred pounds worth, the last time he had been with her, at Glen Ogilvey. . On Dundee's breast they had placed earth, to symbolize the corruptible body, and salt for the immortal spirit.

With all due solemnity, they carried the coffin, turn on turn, over the Banavie Burn, which ran in a deep ravine, with dark trees on the east bank. Up over a low mound they went to the east-end of the Church of Old Blair.

All morning the mourners had trekked from the Red Field to Blair. There a great throng assembled, the air filled with the murmur of subdued conversation. Friends and acquaintances met. There were those who bore wounds, others, who had suffered the loss of relatives or close friends. Many were numb and insensate with the slaughter. Lochiel sought out MacIain; they, the two most elderly Chiefs, to enquire after Iain, to be in turn offered condolences on the loss of his foster son, who had given his life for Lochiel by stepping in front of a Menzie's arrow, which had been intended for the Chief. Each felt the deep ache of regret and bereavement. A silent moment of sad pain.

To the south rose Schehallion's cone, the Fairy Hill; mist hung like a white scarf around its throat. Fitful sunlight shone through the gaps in the clouds. There was no wind. Eastwards, the Castle of Blair, the prize, which had been sought and gained, stood, imperious -------- at what price, now? Butterflies danced, white and dark red. One was caught in a rising thermal and wafted upwards in a rush of air, seen in the frenzy of the instant, almost at once to be lost from sight, to become bewilderingly invisible.

A hiatus of silence developed, when the background sound became that of the Burn and the River Tilt pouring down off the foothills of the Cairngorms, still in raging spate, to be subdued, and quelled, only when they sang the psalm, "The Lord Our God Take Unto You This Your Son"; after which the minister gave them the eulogy,

"From us has gone forth a defiant spirit, one who wore the mantle of command with an easy grace. None could hold a candle to his flame, for it was brighter than a lightning flash, bright and full of magical fire. He has been taken to sit at the Lord's right hand, to bask in the sunshine of His eternal peace. John Graham was a man with an innate sense of justice; to him the personality, which was paramount to his military genius. Most of you here, gathered, to pay tribute, will have many memories of him, for he marched with you, Clan by Clan, joked with you in his halting Gaelic, ate the same food, and slept amongst you, wrapped in a plaid, on the ground. He never shirked a fight, no matter the odds. May God rest him and keep him forever, Iain Dubh nan Cath, Dark John of the Battles".

All prayed, then they sung another psalm. There were those who believed he courted fame in arms, but they were the southrons, the people who did not understand war or the ties of blood or the Clan ethos, people without soul.

Around the grave stood those who had been chosen to take a coffin rope to lower Dundee to his last rest. As the two oldest Chiefs, MacIain and Lochiel had been asked to stand at the head and the feet, the others were Sir Donald MacDonald, Sir John Maclean, Clanranald, Sir Alan Maclean, Glengarry, Keppoch, Dunfermline and Dundee's brother. After they had lowered the coffin Dundee's brother threw the first handful of grave - earth on to the rowan-wood lid. It struck with a hollow echoing sound, followed by the rattle of gravel as it ran, untrammeled, across the wood, seeking to be still. Pitcur, Dundee's old time friend was also laid to rest. MacArthur stepped forward and blew up his pipes and began to play what was to become known as "The Lament for the Viscount Dundee". All about were the best pipers of the Highlands, save MacCrimmon, of whom all there were in awe. A Prince of pipers, for the magical sounds he could produce. They knew that MacArthur was second only to the MacCrimmon, who was God touched.

The chanter's coronach keened, echoing off the Church wall, wailing its woe across the land, sobbing inconsolably. All of the grief of Gaeldom was in the sound, for the man, who, had been the most likely, since the time of the Great Montrose, to lead them to a final victory, which would have allowed the Clan Donald to come into its glory again, and would have given the House of Argyll its just desserts. Weeping notes hung in the air, teardrops of sound, slow melodic pain, sad, yet glorious. There was grief in them like the sighing of an icy wind through the ruined remains of a long deserted croft-house, mournful, and utterly as desolate as the sweetest, most harrowing of hymns, touching all with the essential sadness of life, of the brevity of youth and what passes for beauty, of morality and all earthly joy. Wind arose, with unsummerlike violence, to blow with force against a whinbush , whose last year's seed pods clicked and clacked against the church yard wall in a sudden cacophony of sound. .

A great leader had gone from them, away out to Tir – nan – Og, Land of the Ever Young, to confer with the Great Montrose and Colakiatach and Somerled and Conn of the Hundred Battles.

Many were too stricken to weep. Despair overlaid them. In them was that hollowness, which always lies heavy on a man, after a hard fought battle. Unashamedly, Lochiel wept.

It was a pyrrhic victory, won at such cost. All of the Viscount's greatness had been vaporized to naught. There were those who, in their hearts, knew that, with Ian Dubh nan Cath gone, the Clans, as a fighting entity, were leaderless, for no Chief would own another Chief his master, and, so they would be without direction. Many knew that they had not fought for the King but for Iain Gear Dubh. Now that he was gone the spirit and the drive, for war, was no more.

For several days following the battle Edinburgh was in a state of alarm and many of its inhabitants felt a gut churning fever of fear. The news of the great defeat of the Williamite forces and their total rout was on everyone's lips. Would the Highlanders sweep down on the Town and massacre the populace, with Bloody Claverhouse, the Anti-Christ, the tormentor of the Covenanters, look on, as people were dragged from there homes to be butchered? Hamilton thought of leaving for Clydesdale, Stair wondered if the climate in Galloway might not be kindlier? As ever, the rumor mill was grinding out the distortions of truth, innuendoes and half truths, the creations of the scandal mongers, as fast as its sand-stone wheels would turn. By dribs and drabs, down the whisper stream, the truth came.

Unexpectedly, MacKay,s report of events arrived. At first, as Stair read it, he could not believe it. Then it was borne in on him, Dundee was dead. "This joy I feel, at the news, is like a victory", he exulted. A flush of excitement welled up in him, running through his body. His scalp tingled and the hairs on his head lifted.

XXXIII. THE BOOK AGAIN.

MacKay's offical report of the battle was now in Stair's hands. Carefully he read it. Pausing, now and then, to give consideration to a point, for one thing that his time in Holland had taught him was that Generals, in after battle reports, frequently bent the truth, and seldom listed any of their own mistakes in combat. King William had great trust in MacKay and Stair knew that the King did not like to hear criticism of him. However, he, for his own part, had never liked the man.

With care Stair copied the Report into his Book, word for word, then he appended his own notes. Finally, at pains to see that nothing or no one was missed, he made a detailed list of each Clan, which had been present at Killiecrankie, and of the Chiefs and Sub-Chiefs who had accompanied them.

Then he sat back, a glass of claret to hand, and gave thought to what had passed, and to what was to come. He had no patience with old mens preoccupations with a world that was passing. As usual the Clan Donald was the stumbling block. More and more, it was borne in on him that to achieve the union, with England, which he craved, the savages, of the North, would have to be driven out, or extirpated. This was the one way forward, to peace and prosperity. The snake's head had to be cut off, the Clan Donald had to be made to know that the King was the power in the land, not them. He felt the adrenaline rush of the power game, the most toxic drug of all; to which there was no antidote. To him came the sense of history, of how the past could be made to redispose itself in the future. Seductively the images in his mind turned into a temptation, which insinuated itself, like a vapour, into the closed fortress of his psyche. This was where the vestigial hatreds lurked and the long remembered unrequited wrongs.

If peace could be achieved in Scotland it would release useful numbers of troops to King William, who desperately needed them to fight in the Low Countries. Perhaps he should have a talk on the subject with the Earl of Breadalbane, who, since the execution of Argyll, was the de facto leader of the Clan Campbell, and could, some averred, put seven or eight thousand men under arms, in a fortnight. He also possessed the seven Castles of Barcaldine, Kilchurn, Achallader, Loch Dochart, Edinample, Finlarig and Taymouth, which were spread, in a great chain, across the waist of the Southern Highlands.

XXXIV. DUNKELD.

Colonel Cannon took charge of the Highlanders marching them off north into Aberdeenshire to raid there. Many of the men from the Islands and far-west went with him, in search of further booty, before the long tramp home. There were those, however, who gave him no respect, for he was too much at the aquavitae bottle. Also, he led from behind, unlike Dundee, who had always been in the thick of things.

There were those who left, three or four days after the battle, for it was drawing on to harvest time, or they realised there was no future with Cannon as leader. Dundee had died, the fire was doused.

"Will you be for Glencoe?" Coll of the Cows asked MacIain, his uncle.

"Best I should be for home, to face Mary and let her know of Iain".

"Would it not be better if we went together and took a daunder up the Crooked Glen of the Stones. There's no doubting that we might chance on a cow or two to take home for the winter. What do you say?"

"Temptation it is you are putting in my way, but I like the suggestion, and it will put no distance atal on the journey ".

Coll could tell by his posture, the set of his head, that the old fox had scented blood.

So, it was agreed. No real cattle lifter would let a little problem of provenance get in the way of a quick acquisition.

At Dull there was rolling morning ground fog, whilst cloud and mist folded and moved, refolded and moved again, in a pearl grey sky, which only now and then gave glimpses of the peaks of Carn Mairg and Meall Garbh. The air was soft and heady as undiluted wine.

With no hesitation they began their sweep of the Glen, upwards of three hundred Glencoe and Keppoch MacDonalds. On they went ever west, gathering the livestock and driving it before them. Should plenishings be chanced upon, they were taken, ploughs, candle sticks, agricultural instruments, looms, spinning-wheels, cooking utensils, swees, cogs, harness, blankets, stools, come what may.

By the Lyon they went, the "Tinged River", so called as it was believed the Stewarts of Garth had washed the blood from their hands, in its waters, after a battle. At the tightening throat of the Pass it thundered down through the gorge, funnelled by walls of rock; pulsing like a living artery, a coloured flood, pale gold, fish-belly yellow, and lustrous ochre.

On reaching Chesthill they already had a fair haul of animals taken, but here the numbers increased. So far they had encountered few inhabitants of the Glen, for the women had fled and most of the men were from home.

There was little need for instructions from MacIain or Coll, every man there knew what to do. The pair did not, however let their level of concentration drop. They were ever alert. Both connoisseurs of cattle, supreme among men, who all of their lives had judged the beasts, gathering knowledge of them, through working with them; assessing their worth in an instant, and above all, knowing how to relieve their owners of their right to possess them. Theirs the talent, greater than that of any other Clansman, to lift cattle, and if need be, to take them by stealth or force of arms. They had the nose for it, being able to smell out hidden beasts stanced in a high mountain corrie or other secret places.

Unhurriedly, the breeze came. The mist began to lift, but now and then it hung veil-like across the Glen, soft white, purple and silver grey. Clearer now, a lovely gentle light flooded the ramparts of the Crags. By the Black Wood, where they were startled, on occasions, by the sudden staccato explosion of a tok of cappercailies, bursting through the high leaves. And then they were at Bridge of Balgie. Coll called a halt, as they were nearing Meggernie Castle, where, if they were to be offered any resistance, it was most likely to come.

On the move again they kept as high up the hillsides as they could when they passed the Castle. One or two men could be seen, observing them, from the battlements, but no one sallied forth to confront them.

By evening they had reached the mountain-thirlled lower end of Loch Lyon, which in the fading light gleamed blue as melted sapphire. On the fan of grass, where the river left the loch they put the cattle to graze. Sentries were set out and the Clansmen ate or wrapped themselves in their plaids and went to sleep. At the setting of the sun, for a very few moments, the mountains burned white and red, upon a field of green and gold. The eastern sky grew cold and pale, in the prelude to night. The only sounds were the lowing of cattle and the run of the river. It was as if time had paused.

At first light they took the creich up Glen Meran, down to Achalader and went for Glencoe by Blackmount. Glen Lyon had yielded four hundred cows, nine hundred and sixty sheep, two hundred goats, and thirty-eight horses.

Robert Campbell, Laird of Glen Lyon, in his youth, was handsome and extremely prepossessing. He was well built and tall, with a mass of butter-gold hair and a more pronounced delicacy of face than that of most men. At the Restoration, with its new given freedoms, he burst like a shooting star, into Edinburgh society, a flame clad-lordling, who knew how to dress, for any occasion, and showed the tartan off to good effect. He radiated the self-assurance of a high achiever, in the prime of life. About him was a restless animal vitality. Swiftly he became the matrons' darling. They adored him whilst wishing they were twenty-five years younger. To him it was like escaping from a chrysalis.

Invitations heaped on him, to dances, to go riding on Leith links, to coffee drinking parties, to meets in taverns, to card games, to cock fights. All was a mad whirl, a far cry from the Highland glens. In particular, he quickly came to love card playing, especially where a gamble was involved. It became an obsession. His skill was considerable. Often he would deliberately loose to force the stakes up, then he could win considerable sums of money. One talent, however, he was unable to develop, was to quit when in front. Often he would continue on, after a big win, long into the night, until his stake was gone. Ombre became his favourite game, with its mixture of skill, chance and its call for strong nerves. It had an excitement and demanded great finesse, which fascinated him, though Basset, with much less skill requirement, had its appeal, for of all games, with odds of sixty four to one, the gains could be stupendous, though the losses, which a true gambler seldom considered, were severely punitive.

Gradually the amounts of money lost and owing had grown to the extent that Glenlyon had to leave Edinburgh, to return to his estate at Megernie. However, with his boundless charm he had won the hand of Helen Lindsay, an heiress of considerable means. At once he began an extensive programme of repairs and improvements to Megernie Castle. In three years, the building work completed, all of his wife's money, and more, was spent. He was virtually penniless, afloat on a sea of debt. Eventually, he embraced a two-fold solution.

First, he took to drinking, which he found dissolved the doubts in his mind, honing away the roughness, implanting a smoothness with no need to look to the future, and, best of all, no reckoning, with a blurring of the edges of his conscience.

Second, he appealed to the grandees of Clan Campbell, with respect to his straitened circumstances. They answered his call by setting up a committee controlled by the young Argyll and the Laird of Glenorchy, the two most powerful members of the Clan, to administer his affairs. With an eye ever to the future, Glenorchy made sure that all of the documents relating to Glenlyon passed through his office, seen only by himself or his Chamberlain. At first Glenlyon was hard put to it to keep body and soul together for several winters; he and his family nearly starving to death, living in extreme want. Indeed, if it had not been for the charity of some of his tenants and kindness shown him by members of the Clan he and his family would not have survived.

In the fullness of time the Laird of Glenorchy was minded to carry out an invasion of the lands of Sinclair, Earl of Caithness, whom he had enmeshed in debt over the years, with a bond on all of his lands, property and titles .Of all of the Highland Chiefs he, alone, had brought this type of ensnarement to almost an art form, For him it was fascinating, intriguing, with often considerable reward. Down the years he had come to believe that in pursuing money or possessions there were no rules. You took what you could get any way you could. He persuaded Glenlyon to lead the invasion into Caithness, and to take out a bond for five thousand pounds to finance the incursion. This operation was hugely successful and resulted in Glenorchy becoming the Earl of Caithness. This title, Charles the Second, for reasons of policy, returned to the Sinclairs, and in its place, Glenorchy was created Earl of Breadalbane and Holland.

At a stroke the MacDonalds, with the great Creich, totally ruined Glenlyon. Darkness came upon his soul and often he wept; tears of ice fell from his eyes and grief engulfed him. No one could find words to console him for the complete destruction of his world. They did not exist. Conflict marched across his face, there was despair and a deep well of frustration, which flowed from the vision of his descent into ignominy and ridicule; his mouth was filled with the vinegar of disgrace.

Later desperation forced him to sell many of the woods on his lands. When the loggers felled the two and three hundred year old forests of fragrant pine, at the toppling of an ancient tree, clothed with plates of red bark, which had waited on time with supreme patience, tears would come, unbidden, to his eyes.

Finally, there was no other recourse, he had to dispose of his estate to Athol.

Finished raiding in Aberdeenshire Cannon marched south for Dunkeld, which was held by the Cameronian Regiment, under William Clelland. Here he was met by fierce resistance as the houses were well defended and it was impossible to employ the charge. Though Clelland was killed the Cameronians fought doggedly on, until at the point of defeat, the Highlanders, short of ammunition, unused to this type of fighting, turned about and marched off. It was in effect an end to the war.

Through the influence of Breadalbane, Glenlyon was commissioned as a Captain in Argyll's Regiment of Foot. He was now wholly dependent on his soldier's pay to support his family, and deeper in Breadalbane's debt

A fortnight after he returned MacIain had news of the fate of his son. Colonel Hill sent word that Iain had been taken prisoner and was now lodged in prison in Glasgow. Again and then again the Chief read Hill's letter. Each time he felt a little more joy, a lightening of the spirit. He knew that Iain would not take to the prison regime, but he was alive, not buried in some unmarked grave or lost in the vastness of the great waters of the Northern Ocean.

William was in the Low Countries conducting his war, whilst his wife, Queen Mary was in London, with full authority to handle affairs in Britain as she thought fit. It was brought to her attention that a small number of Highlanders, who had been captured at Killiecrankie, were languishing in Scottish Jails. At once she took steps to have them freed, signing the release documents herself. In the main she was driven by sentiment, for she knew that the Clans had been very supportive to her father, and, back down the years, to the Stuarts. There was also the consideration that it was costly to finance their imprisonment and that their liberation would give rise to, perhaps, more affection for the new Royals.

XXXV. ACHALLADER.

Looking for a less troublesome Highland region King William issued a commission to Breadalbane to treat with the Clans to see if they could be brought to heel. But, this proved to be more difficult than had been thought. Not a single Chief was willing to give his allegiance to the Government. Frustration built in both Breadalbane and the King, that no conclusion could be reached. Reports, between them and Melville and Stair, the Secretaries of State, shuttled back and forth, between the Low Countries, London, Edinburgh and the Highlands. At last it was decided that the best course would be for Breadalbane to meet the Chiefs at a suitable venue, somewhere in the Highlands. At once Breadalbane suggested it take place at his castle of Achallader, it being best sited for the Clansmen to travel to without especially long journeys. It was agreed that the conference should be called for June.

Close on five hundred came to Achallader. Each Chief had his" tail", his chosen men, to accompany him. His Piper, his Purse Bearer, his Sword Carrier, the Clan Bard and others as they saw fit. To be within the circle of a Clan Chief's patronage was to be one of the elite.

All around the castle tents were erected. Food and ale for all was at hand. Those who were there, but would not be involved in the negotiations, treated it as a festival and enjoyed themselves.

In the Hall, the Chiefs met, to be addressed by Breadalbane, to see what was on offer, and to make the best deal possible. There had been prior hints of money, nothing hard and fast, just a word here and a word there, to whet the appetite. Perhaps? Perhaps?

He opened with words of welcome. His collar was of the finest Flemish lace, his waistcoat was of green velvet with on it leaping embroidered golden stags, which toned well with his dark green tartan trews. MacIain saw how deceptive were his myopic eyes, set in a pale face, for which men called him Iain Glas, Sallow John. This indeed was a very formidable man. To look on him was to be conscious of the power, the enormous drive, and the quest for domination that lived within him. He also bore the gene, which his ancestors had passed down to him, stronger than that possessed by any other living Campbell, that of land-hunger. To him land was all, the possession of it a total sickness, bane to the soul, which, most of all the Campbells of Glenorchy knew. It was a form of lust, a disease, an obsession, uncontrollable and almost incapable of being satisfied.

"King William, who has appointed me to bring about a peace in the Highlands, extends his welcome to you. He is aware of your concerns and acknowledges that you had past loyalties to James. However, he wishes to stress to you all, that he is now the sovereign King and as such calls for your loyalty to him, and him alone. As a mark of his good faith he has entrusted to me the sum of twelve thousand pounds, to be distributed in such a way as to allow Chiefs, who are beholden to feudal superiors, to buy out their indebtedness".

There was a great shuffling of feet and the volume of conversation swelled to fill the hall.

Locheil, who had previously been chosen as spokesmen for the Chiefs, rose."We have come here, all in good faith, to hear what the Government proposes. How do you, the spokesman for William of Orange, intend to proceed?"

All, there, noted that Locheil had not used the word "King".

"It is my intention to talk with each Chief, on his own, to establish what each individual has in mind, for himself and for the general good"

"That is as maybe", said Lochiel."However, if any Chief finds that he is discomfited with the suggestion, or if he feels uncomfortable during the course of the talk alone, with yourself, we would ask that the person involved should be free to break off, without any prejudice accruing to that person ".

"That is acceptable. However, at the outset, when I said "alone", my Chamberlain will be in attendance for the purpose of taking notes on the proceedings".

No one objected.

In all it took three and a bit days for the interviews. No Chief was willing to take the Indemnity before another did so. However, what Breadalbane gleaned from the discussions was that money was uppermost in most mens' minds and the catholic Chiefs were very averse to swearing the oath. Secretly Breadalbane worried that greed might cloud his judgement. He could not let them have an inkling of his desire to bank the money earmarked for them, now could he? Some of it he resolved he would have, how much remained to be seen.

As MacIain entered the Hall the chill of Highland acrimony struck him instantly. Nearly always it was about the possession or disposition of cattle or land. It was the coldest of all colds, frequently more divisive than politics or religion. It could start feuds and continue them for eternity, or until death, by nature or the sword, gave the final decision. For years the two men had been enemies, worse still in Glencoe's mind was that this was a Campbell, whilst Breadalbane, on the other hand, had lost many cattle over the years, and men as well. The lands of Glencoe, which intruded deep into his territory, were ever a thorn in his flesh.

What stakes was Breadalbane playing for? Twelve thousand pounds? A Dukedom? The Chieftainship of Clan Campbell? Who knew? Only he himself knew, or did he want them all? So much was happening here, so many nuances, so many undercurrents. The Chief, over the years, had come to the conclusion, that the Laird of Glenorchy, was fed by an unending lust for power, that could never be sated.

Barcaldine, the Chamberlain, looked on. The two Chiefs were, for all the world, like stags at the rut, taking each the measure of the other, not locking antlers, but posturing, stiff necked, all seeing. Tension hung, so palpable that you could have cut it with a knife. Unable to help himself Breadalbane was on the attack straight away.

"There is the matter, which has never been cleared up of the fight at Stronclachan, where you and yours left eighteen of my men dead. Also, lately, three of your men lifted cows out of Glenstrae. How do you intend to compensate for my losses?" Between them the question hung like a clear drop of water ready to fall into a dark pool.

"Surely there are more important things to be talked on", retorted MacIain. For the matter of the three men you mention, they were outlawed from Glencoe six years ago and have never been back since. As far as I know they serve Campbell of Ardchattan, and he should answer for them. Regards Stronclachan, my men were about their peaceful business of fishing for salmon, when they were ordered off the river by your Campbells. On refusal your men drew swords and started the fight. It is regrettable that eighteen of your men were slain, but six MacDonalds died and five were sore hurt. A man has the right to defend himself when attacked. Yours should not have drawn sword".

Heat entered the Earl's voice, "You and yours are forever thieving. Come what may, these matters are still to be brought to a conclusion, you are assured of that". His words hung in the air, malevolent, full of portent and menace, the spitting whisper of the serpent. He liked declarations of war. They gave life a certain edge. Particularly, if in an hour or two you could put a thousand warriors into the field, when the opponent, at a push, could not muster more than a hundred and fifty.

MacIain could feel the meeting coming to a rapid and unsatisfactory conclusion. He could also see that they were very near to blows, and at a meeting of Chiefs that would never do. So, even with the future now filled with uncertainty, MacIain raised himself to his full nineteen and three quarter hands in height, turned on his heel and strode from the room.

At the next meeting, with all present, Lochiel rose. "I speak for the other Chiefs. We have discussed what you have said and as a result we have counter proposals for you. They ask that all of the expenses incurred in the Highland War, the sum of twenty thousand pounds should be made good to them. Also, we have ascertained the sums required, by each, to pay off the feudal superiorities; the list we will pass to your Chamberlain for him to note. Further, all men should have a full indemnity and be allowed to continue to bear arms. Finally, emissaries should be sent to France to obtain James's permission before any oath taking is entered into".

Breadalbane was much more conciliatory, using a less direct and forceful approach, perhaps as a result of his findings, as to attitudes, over the last three days. His speech was liquid flowing Gaelic, of which any bard would have been proud. To MacIain's ears the sentences dripped off his tongue like heather honey from a scone. His words had gloss and altered emphasis. With skill he picked out an individual here, an individual there, larding them with flattery, cunningly persuasive. He was at ease with words. He made great play of the King's wish to see that men should be made free of their monetary burdens to others, and that William was their friend.

At once MacIain's mind was filled with the thought of all of the people who were thirled to Breadalbane by debts due, on bonds, on land, which the Earl had bought up, becoming, in all of the nation, the undoubted master of this form of transaction. "Perish the thought".

Then the Earl subtly, almost unnoticed, let it be known, that he really was a Jackobite at heart. He had entered the Government only for the purpose of undermining it from within. Also, he claimed that a settlement would result in the dismantling of the hated Fort William, which General MacKay had just re- built.

This was too much for the man from Glencoe. He uncoiled off his seat to stand. He blew down through his nostrils, like a bull, fierce and proud, now highly irate.

"Who here will listen to this man? I tell you all, now, he speaks to you with the split tongue of a snake. In the Highlands he is King James's man, in Edinburgh he is the Prince of Orange's man. Can you not see the layers of pretence curling back like the bark on a birch log when it is laid wet on the fire? " Anger rippled through his words and seemed to crackle like summer lightning at the ends of his hair. With no more ado he stormed out of the Hall to seek comfort in the wind and the rain.

Saying not a word he motioned to his two sons, gathered his followers about him with a movement of his hand. For once he paid no attention to his deerhounds. Bran raised his great head and looked at his Master, his eyes taking all in, Luath stood, a carved slate statue, with a scatter of white hairs along his flanks and a white blaze on his chest. Grianne, the bitch, uncomprehending, tucked her tail between her legs, went down on her belly, inched forward slowly, whining softly all the while. Without a pause MacIain swung up on to his garron, and was off for Glencoe. Stiffly he sat the horse, his posture speaking the after-shock of his anger.

Low –toned, a curlew cried. Its liquid music the embodiment of the spirit of the wild moors and lonely trackless places.

To keep himself in the forefront of things Breadalbane sailed for Flanders to consult with the King. Indeed, he was well received, better than he had expected. It was apparent that William wished for a settled Highlands, his greatest need being more troops for Flanders. Adroitly Breadalbane turned the conversation to his Castle of Kilchurn, where he had already started to build a huge additional barrack block, capable of accommodating two hundred men. He put it to the King that he could form a militia of four thousand, to police the North, the headquarters to be Kilchurn, with himself as General. There was no doubt that the idea had appeal for William, but there were reservations. He informed Breadalbane that he would need to consult General MacKay before coming to any conclusion. Also, William, though he kept the thought to himself, was cautious as to allowing the powerful Clan Campbell to have even more power.

Well pleased with his trip Breadalbane took ship back to England, arriving in London in mid September. There, news awaited him that not a single Chief had taken indemnity. He had expected that at least one or two would have done so in his absence. In his heart he knew that the trouble was that no Chief wanted to be the first to agree.

On King William's order the Privy Council issued a proclamation promising indemnity and full restoration to favour of all rebels, who took the oath by the first of January

As it drew on into winter Breadalbane continued to have informal discussions with the Chiefs, with no real progress being made. Also, he continued with building at Kilchurn, despite running up considerable debts by doing so.

On the third of October the Treaty of Limerick was signed, effectively ending the war in Ireland. William was overjoyed for this meant that he would have an army to deploy in the Low Countries, the following spring. But he was still needed a further four regiments from Scotland.

Following the meeting at Kilchurn, which had produced no results, Breadalbane wrote to Stair suggesting that the time had now arrived when an example should be shown to act as a deterrent to the Highlanders. He used the phrase "mauling in the winter nights", and recommended that the Clan Donald should be targeted. For his part Stair was receptive now, determined on a permanent settlement, being furious at the "unreliable" Chiefs, as he felt they threatened his position and besides they were rebels. His Presbyterianism surfaced. "All the Papist Chiefs stand forefaulted by acts of Parliament, and this should be enforced. Glengarry and Keppoch are Catholic and as such should be extirpated to vindicate the King's justice". His was an indifference as to how the settlement was achieved, as long as it was brought to a conclusion. Cut off the snake's head and show the Clan Donald that the King was the power in the land, not them. Rules did not count for much, this was the Highlands, there was no law. His quill spat ink like snake venom as he carved his rage into the parchment he wrote upon.

Things did not go well for the Joint Secretary of State Melville, inexorably, slowly, as a single drips of water, falling from a cave roof, at long intervals, erodes soluble limestone, his authority began to leach away. One could not say that there was a single reason for its going, but subtly it was happening. There were religious difficulties, which at any time are not easy to solve. King William was also troubled by the swings in political influence, which Melville seemed to be unable to curb, for he had the desire not to permit one faction to become dominant.

Power and the need for it was a narcotic in Stairs blood, stronger than the poppy or the finest bottle of claret. He was fully aware that leadership brought with it awesome and inescapable responsibilities of life and death. He also saw that with Melville's decline the time was coming when he would be Sole Secretary of State, the time when he would be the ultimate power behind the throne. Already, he had dreams as to the future. His hope was that his political career would culminate in the control of the nation's destiny. His was the comprehension of the dynamics of political infighting, which no other of the time had. He understood the needs and uses of power, and, above all else he had the knowledge, that before all others, he had the comprehension which would result in the coming to power, as his right, for he knew it was to him alone, to no other,

In the first week of December Melville was dismissed. Now Stair had come into his own. What he savoured was the marriage of jurisprudence and power; in his mind the perfect consummation. The moment was the culminating point for two different men, with two different careers, now starkly merged. Stair the lawyer, hot for the Presbyterian religion, with the total belief that he was the person to unite the Kingdoms, to give them peace and prosperity, and having the talent, possessed by few men, to act without remorse. William of Orange, the Statholder, the Prince of the Netherlands, the man who had stood against the might of Europe, who had united the Low Countries under his banner, and whose most pressing need was for troops to fight on the Continent.

With care Dalrymple considered how best to use Breadalbane. There was no doubt that his knowledge of Highland affairs and the influence he could wield north of the Highland Line was enormous. There was also the enmity between Hill, Governor and Commanding Officer of Fort William, and Breadalbane, to be taken into account, stemming from the Earl's wish that Kilchurn be made the chief post in the North, which threatened Hill's position, and the fact that Hill was now in possession of letters which purported to show Breadalbane's Jackobite leanings.

Dalrymple could see advantage in the situation. He had little doubt that he could persuade King William that the letters were false, but, in doing so he would make Breadalbane even more beholden to him. The Earl for his part was keeping a low profile, preferring to stay on his own estates and on no account to venture to Edinburgh, pleading his old complaint "of the gout".

From a completely unexpected quarter, Dalrymple received a communication. Lieutenant Colonel James Hamilton, The Assistant Governor and Second in Command of Fort William, wrote to him expressing his doubts as to the seeming lack of funding reaching the Garrison, and expressing the hope that the moneys intended were not finding their way to Kilchurn?

Quickly, Dalrymple responded, ensuring Hamilton that in no way would any finance or supplies needed be diverted to Breadalbane. He also added that he would welcome the Assistant Governor's views on a campaign against the rebel Clan Donald, in particular

Glengarry? In the knowledge that Hamilton was an Irish Protestant refugee Dalrymple was aware he would have no scruples about moving against Catholic enemies, who, as he put it, were destroying the very fabric of civilisation.

From an entry previously noted in "The Book" Dalrymple had the seeds of an idea sown. "Yes", he thought, "perhaps now is the time to put to use Breadalbane's placement of his kinsman Glenlyon, as Captain in Argyll's Regiment of Foot?" Indeed enquiries yielded the information that Glenlyon, as Commander of a Company, was based at Stirling Castle. Though the oldest man now serving there he was looked upon as a fine officer. A carefully worded letter also elicited from Breadalbane the fact that Glenlyon was, in every way, still under obligation to Breadalbane; though the Secretary of State knew from his years in the Law and Politics, that gratitude was the least lasting of virtues. His father had drummed it into him. "Do not count on the gratitude of deeds done for people, in the past. You must make them grateful for the things you will do for them in the future".

Had not Cicero, in a speech to the Senate, when speaking of Julius Caesar, said, *"Great men buy their own goodwill, forgiveness for betraying friends and exercising lethal judgements"*.

XXXVI. The White Stag.

"I hear tell that a white stag has been seen on the Blackmount Hills. Would you be thinking that we might have a try for it?"

Callum looked at his twin brother. "So you have heard of it too. We would have to be careful, for where it runs is ground claimed by Breadalbane, and I have no doubt he would not take kindly to the lifting of a stag, particularly a white one".

They were so alike, identical twins. In fact the only difference, if one knew where to look, was that Callum was right handed and Duncan left handed. They were known as Callum nam Fiadh and Duncan Kiotach nam Fiadh, Callum of the Deer and Left Handed Duncan of the Deer.

"It would have to be a stalk, no dogs, up on it, one shot of the gun and then away with haste. There might be no time for the gralloch before it was got on the garron's back, which would mean that it would be a heavy lift for us, up on to the horse, and a greater burden for it than usual".

"Aye, that sounds about right. The extra thirty pounds you and I can manage, but it will be sore on the garron, for where it would have to carry the beast is amongst the hardest country to take a deer out of, very steep and rocky".

"Perhaps, it would be best if we were to go and have a look at the ground first", said Callum.

"So, you are up for it then?"

There was no need of an answer, they each knew that the other wanted to take the stag, no matter the difficulties. Besides was it not in the hills claimed, as his, by Breadalbane, which made it all the more desirable?

In three days they had surveyed the ground. There were plenty of deer, but they did not see a white stag. However they had found six or seven places where they could leave the pony, well hidden, whilst they were at the stalk, with ample grass to keep it content. Also they had noted where the shielings were sited, for they knew it was best to steer clear of people, especially Campbells.

A fortnight later they were back. For five days they covered the ground assiduously but there was not a single sighting of the quarry.

"Callum, I am thinking that maybe the white stag is gone or even that it was only in peoples' imaginations. Would we not be better to be going home, for there is that field of corn still to be gathered?"

"Seeing we are here let's have one more day. Maybe we will be lucky?"

"Right then, the morn we'll be at it early".

In the dead hour before dawn they had stanced the garron in a secluded spot, on a long rope, so that it could feed as it chose. Then they climbed fast, up the steep side of Meall Tarsuinn till they were to the left of Corrie Riabhach and about five hundred feet below its rim. All at once the mountains were bathed in the rich pink glow of dawn. As the day came, the high tops, in the early sunlight, gleamed like precious jewels. Soft ruby, delicate sapphire, and lustrous pearl, painted like a peacock's tail, in a fanfare of colour.

With care Callum unpacked his eye- glass from its case and began the slow careful sweep from left to right, then back again, searching, each time, lower down into the corrie, looking for deer.

Duncan cursed, under his breath, for an eagle had just flown over, on the lookout for its breakfast. It tilted left, sideslipping through the air with effortless ease, its wings motionless, except for the extended emarginated primary feathers at the tips, which flexed and moved incessantly. It rode the air, replete with power, passing over its kingdom, at some eighty miles per hour. Then it was gone. Duncan breathed a sigh of relief, for even full- grown deer will often panic as an eagle flies over. Perhaps a residual memory implanted in their minds since they were young calves?

Scree stone slithered on the slope with a soft sibilant hiss as four hinds made their way over it, the only animals, which could do so with impunity, with no fear for their safety. Heads up in that lovely elegance of astonishment Movement ran through them, subtle and tentative, totally enchanting. They scattered and were gone. Five minutes later the scree stone rattled again as over the shoulder came two stags and three hinds. The lead stag was young, an eight pointer, but the other was a royal of twelve points, majestic, in his prime, the colour of the drifts, on Rannoch Moor, of the mystic canna bawn, the bobbing white heads of bog cotton. Both men had seen it. Instantly, they felt the adrenaline surge burning in their blood, like a clean bright flame. They had seldom felt so alert.

For no apparent reason the deer started off, drifting cloud shadows, moving swiftly over the chutes of stone, all wild, indescribable grace. In a heart- beat they were quarter of a mile away.

Callum rose, no need to stay concealed now, for they were over the shoulder and upwind. Movement, if they saw you, would spook them, but, if the breeze was from man to them, they would scent you at up to two miles distant. However, Callum had checked previously how the air was moving and knew that it was favourable.

The white stag had broken from the others and gone straight up the steep slope, whilst the hunters waited below, out of sight of him, but he had turned off at right angles amongst the peat hags on the high ground. Then he had gone into a burn, as if he intended to climb up its course. Unknown to its pursuers, he had turned in the stream, where no tracks would be left to betray him, and gone downhill. Duncan and his brother went straight down, making good time and using every inch of cover they could find, but they discovered that they had overshot his trail. Once more the stag had doubled back and waded up a smaller burn, before again going off at right angles.

By chance Duncan happened to see antlers protruding above a small hillock of moss; whereupon, the men had to rest, for crawling on hands and knees, on very difficult terrain, through icy water courses, or the glaur of glutinous peat bogs, with sharp stones tearing at clothes and bare skin, had fatigued them, making a pause necessary to allow the senses to recover sufficiently, before a shot was taken.

Slowly Callum unslung the gun from his back, checked the condition of the powder in the firing pan and blew on the smouldering end of the match-tow, until it glowed red. At fifty paces he knew that the beast was at extreme range. Nevertheless, because of the lie of the land he also knew that they could not get closer, or the deer would be up and away. He sighted on the neck, knowing that, as the stag was downhill, he must aim high. Quietly he let his breath out, steadied himself and fired.

Instantly, the stag was up and running flat out. For a hundred yards it went at full gallop, then, just as suddenly, it crumpled and fell in a heap.

Duncan let out a yell and at once was off at full tilt, knife in hand. His brother was left to secure the gun and the eyeglass. When he came up with Duncan they both spent some time examining the deer.

"As there is no one about I think we should gralloch it. The lesser weight will help the garron"

So they did so, eviscerating it, removing the offal from the body. Within five minutes a pair of ravens had arrived, a lustrous sparkling black. They had not seen them previously, but wily and knowing, as all of their kind, they always seemed able to arrive immediately the gralloch was started. Tradition had made it the established practice for the G20llocher to provide "the Ravens'Share". They sidled forward, watching the men from the sides of their eyes, and began to feed.

With no need to hurry now, but anxious to be off home, Callum brought up the pony and they loaded it with the carcass of the stag.

"Man, but is not time we were having that wee dram?"

So they did, from Duncan's ramshorn flask

They savoured it, toasting "The White Stag".

"A dram of the whisky, at the right time, and if it's the right stuff, can work more miracles than a church full of saints", enthused Callum.

"I am thinking, may be Angus nan Oran, Angus of the Songs, MacIain's brother, who is the poet, will do a verse on the White Stag?"

"Well, we'll wait and see?"

Both knew that if a bard composed a verse it would run round the Highlands and enhance their already considerable reputation as deer hunters.

Lower down the going was easier. One or two of the hills were still wearing the royal purple of the heather, but most were beginning to sport the rust of dying bracken. Birches, which were on the heights, were already golden, though those on the lower ground were multi-hued green and myriad shades of yellow. As they passed through a narrow defile they were, suddenly, surrounded by a ring of sixteen men. At once they knew them, by their tartan, as Breadalbane's. Resistance was impossible, as was flight. They had their hands bound, then they began the trek to Kilchurn, where they were warded in the castle's bottle dungeon. There, to await Breadalbane's pleasure. He being absent, away to Finlarig, on Loch Tayside.

How long they were in the dungeon they could not tell for there it was pitch dark. Only now and then there was a glimmer of daylight, when food was lowered to them, which was quickly doused when the iron grating clanged shut and the trapdoor above it was closed. At last the Earl returned and they were dealt with.

A week later they were back in Glencoe. At a single stroke Breadalbane had, forever, eased the problem of identifying which twin was which? Also from that time forth each had a new name, Duncan One-ear and Callum Lugless, for the Earl had had their ears cropped; both of Callum's and one of Duncan's. Where they had been removed, in the same plane as their jaw lines, there were livid, wrinkled holes, ravaged pits, surrounded by still healing scar tissue.

"I am thinking that it would be best if the poem on the White Stag was composed by Iain Lom, Sarcastic John, for he has no love atal for the Campbells. Angus nan Oran would not be making it nearly as strong", said Callum.

XXXVII.
THE SECOND SIGHT.

With suddenness the rain had come on just as they had topped the rise up from Loch Tulla. Now, after a further five miles Alasdair and his three companions were soaked to the skin. All were miserable and chilled to the bone. What a relief to enter the Pass down into Glencoe! Beneath the lowering clouds not a hill was visible, though following the track was easy, as they had done so, time after time, day or night.

"I could be using a drink", said Archie. "How about us stopping in to see if Fergus Taish has any whisky?"

In his mind Alasdair was loth to do so, but he held his tongue, for he could see his companions were fatigued and a drink would be welcome to them. For his own part he did not much care for Fergus, whom he considered to be a drunk, and he had no regard for his reputation as the foremost of the Taishatrin, those of the Second Sight, in the Glen. He, Alasdair, unlike many, had no feel for superstition, treating it with disdain, even though, a year before, the Seer had warned MacIain of an ambush, to come, which had saved his father's life.

Still, the whisky, when it was poured, was good. It put warmth and juice back into their bodies. Their host seemed to be, as usual, in an alcoholic haze. He consumed his drink with an appalling deliberation. Perhaps, the fire of it helped him to face his demons and life as well?

Anxious to be on his way, before his friends became the worse of wear, Alasdair thanked Fergus for his hospitality and made ready to be off.

"I'll be having a word with you, yourself, for I have a message for Himself, your father, which I am thinking you should tell him of".

"What was it now? Best to humour the old fool".

" Tell MacIain, that, when the white shroud of the snow is on the ground, he should have a care of him whom had held the nine of diamonds in his hand".

In the weeks to come the Chief's son never told his father of the conversation with the Seer, for why should he trouble him with the wanderings, of the delirium, of a drink befuddled mind?

XXXVIII. THE OATHTAKING.

There seemed to be no sense of urgency with James at St. Germain. Menzies became more and more frustrated. Would the man ever sign the papers to free the Chiefs from their oath of allegiance? More pressing was the fact that time was leaking away. Each day that passed was a day less for the Clansmen to swear to William of Orange. With the nearing of the first of January, Menzies was conscious of the ever-opening trapdoor, through which the Chiefs would fall if they did not take the Oath; soon, very soon, it would be a yawning gap. That James was dilatory, none could deny.

At last it came, the letter, signed by James, instructing the Chiefs to proceed, as they thought fit, to take whatsoever steps that they found necessary for their safety. It bore the date the second of December.

Immediately, Menzies started off on his journey back to Scotland, as he knew how short was the time remaining. By the fifth he had taken ship at Dunkirk.

Now, as Sole Secretary of State Dalrymple alone had King William's ear.

"Sire, in the matter of the Highlands, it is not so much a frighteningly dangerous godliness which is sweeping the land, but an anarchy of lawlessness, which, I am of the opinion, will only respond to violent extirpation, which must be total, with not a single iota left to cause further taint. It must, to be effective, be complete". Full of portent the words hung in the air.

By now the Secretary knew that, in all probability, there would not be a prompt reply from the King, for William was given to letting matters slide, pertaining to Scotland. But, in this instance the response was immediate.

"So far, despite all of our best efforts, these Rebels, I call them so unreservedly, have seen fit not to come to terms with all of our best efforts to achieve a peace with them. Therefor we must proceed against them now, for the imperative is for a submission, which will release troops, to fight in Flanders, in the spring, for the plans for our offensive against the French are much advanced. In which case you should put in hand the necessary orders for the use of military force, as is deemed to be required".

On the fifteenth the Order to proceed with the winter campaign was given. It was envisaged that a two pronged operation would be used, with troops moving down the Great Glen from Inverness, and a force from Fort William being employed. Glengarry was the target. Cunningly Dalrymple had not consulted the Privy Council, as he knew their were those on it who would have spoken out at military proceedings against the Clans.

Off Dover, on the crossing from France, which had been sorely troubled by weather, the Emissaries must have felt a terrible desolation of the spirit. Sir George Barclay, overwhelmed, hurled his grief at the sky, tempered with a larding of oaths, for, they were apprehended by an English warship, and then taken, as prisoners to London.

In all they were interrogated and held, by the authorities, until the seventeenth of December, when only Menzies was released, after taking an oath to King William. Sir George refused, point blank, to do the same. So, in desperate haste Menzies made his way to Scotland alone. By the twenty- second, in an exhausted state, he reached his home, just east of Dunkeld. Without hesitation, before he ate, though he did have a stiff brandy, he had his clerk begin the work of producing copies of King James's letter, which freed the Chiefs from allegiance. By that evening they were on the way to the more distant Chiefs, the remainder being despatched the next day.

On Christmas Day Robert Campbell of Glenlyon left Stirling Castle, with his troops, to march to Dunstaffnage, where they were to be based, as Fort William was already filled to overflowing. On the way north they went via Glenlyon, where Robert had a private meeting with Breadalbane. No other person was present.

It was late, on the last day of December, when MacIain rode up to the gate of Fort William. Darkness was coming. There was a lurid orange patch in the western sky and heavy clouds were beginning to disperse. The wind was dropping and a star or two twinkled through the chinks. Facing west the heaviest cannon stood in a half moon, just where MacKay had placed them, to repel any attack from the sea. Gulls flew, beating away west, their cries forlorn in the air.

Quickly the Officer of the Guard led the Clansman, at his request, to Colonel Hill, the Commander, who greeted him cordially; they being long time friends. Indeed MacIain had, many years before, taught the Governor how to fish for salmon in the River Leven.

"What brings you here, at this late hour, MacIain? Will you have a bite to eat?"

"That I will, though the reason I am here is to take the oath to King William".

"Man, that is unfortunate for, even though I am the Governor, I have not the legal authority to administer it. Did no-one tell you that it must be sworn before a Sheriff?"

Nonplussed MacIain was for the moment speechless.

"But that will mean going to Ardkinglas, at Inverary, and there is no way I can be there before the stated time".

"Have some food and, whilst you are at your meal I will pen a letter to Ardkinglas explaining that mistakenly you came here prepared to take the oath. That should stand you in good stead with the Sheriff.

In an hour the old Colonel was as good as his word and the letter was ready.

"Will you not stay the night for it has just started to snow? You are more than welcome".

"Perhaps then I will do so if you have the guard wake me an hour before first light, in the morning. Then I will be off without disturbing yourself. I thank you for you help and for the letter"

There was only a faint glimmer of light when MacIain and his companions set off. As the day lightened they saw that a layer of new fallen snow covered everything, the whiteness stretching away into nothingness. Overall lay the heavy silence that it had brought with it. With close on eighty miles of trackless waste to cross MacIain knew that he had a hard road to face. A sense of vague, all-encompassing despair seeped into him. He was filled with foreboding.

During the night he had made up his mind as to how he meant to proceed. There was no sense what ever in going into the lion's den roaring, no sense to draw unwanted attention, as he surely would in going to Inverary, the very heartland of Clan Campbell; in which case he would dispense with his tail of followers, sending all but two of them back to Glencoe, when they reached the nearest point to it. Better to be circumspect. This was not the time to have his Piper march before him playing his pipes down the main street of the Campbells' town, with his Purse Bearer, Sword Boy and others trailing behind. At Invercoe, though they were loth to go, he sent the men home, keeping Achtriachtan's son and Angus with him. There was no let up in the snowfall; the quilt of it thickening as it came in large flakes, wet and pure. Steel cold the air, in a glass shard wind.

At Benderloch, just before they were to turn off and go over the hill for Bonawe, suddenly, as they came through a copse of silver birch trees, they were confronted by a troop of redcoats, soldiers who obviously meant business, muskets presented.

"In the name of King William we ask who you are and what business you have on the road?" a mounted officer demanded.

"I am MacIain of Glencoe, just come from Colonel Hill, at Fort William, where I was about the taking of the oath to the King"

"Get down from your horse".

At once the Chief complied, for he could see little else he could do.

With no offered explanation as to why they were apprehended they were escorted to Barcaldine Castle, one of Breadalbane's seven fortresses. There, at once, they were interrogated by Captain Thomas Drummond of Argyll's Regiment. He was very correct and direct in his questioning, though MacIain felt a tiny glimmer of suspicion gnawing at the back of his head, the flow of the language and the way in which it was couched made him wonder if some of it may not have been rehearsed? Had Hamilton, the Assistant Governor at Fort William. had a hand in it?

Confident of possessing a trump card MacIain produced his letter from Colonel Hill. Drummond read it slowly, obviously considering every word.

"Very interesting ", he said finally, "but how am I to know if it is a forgery or not?"

"God's Blood man, do you not recognise he signature of the Governor of the Fort?"

There was no reply from Drummond. He looked up at the Chief, a hint of a smile passed across his face, perhaps, of mild cynicism, like a breeze. Without further ado he instructed the escort to "put MacIain in the press".

For the night, that was indeed where he lodged, under a stairway, in a cupboard, which had a stout door, and two guards posted outside. Angus and Triachtan Og were locked in a freezing cold outhouse, though all were fed and given ale to drink. In the morning they were all set free, much to their surprise. For, early on, a boat had come down Loch Linnhe, from Fort William, and Captain Drummond had been left, in no uncertain doubt, that the Governor had indeed written and signed the letter to Ardkinglas, and that, all had better be aware of the fact, that safe passage was to be given to MacIain, Chief of Glencoe.

At once they were off south, up on to the heights for Bonawe, through drifts where men and garrons floundered, often causing the riders to dismount and lead the horses. It was tough going, even for these men, who were inured to hardship, for the cold was penetrating. In beauty wind sculpted drifts lay all around, but they did not see them, for they were intent only on pressing on for Inverary. At times, unbidden, the wind would rise, halooing like a lost shade, driving the flakes into their faces, chilling their eyes. By Loch Aweside they went, the great expanse of it, stretching away before them, flecked with wind spume, and, in places, where sheltered by the land, the snow water lay, a sheet of green glass, without flaw.

At Cladich they struck up and over the hill for Glen Aray. Triachtan Og, though he knew better than to say it, was concerned for the old Chief for the grey patina of fatigue was on his skin.

At last, all worn out, they reached Inverary town. No one was about, all storm-bound in their homes.

"I would trust nobody, not in this pit of snakes", Triachtan Og said, distaste in his voice.

"Hold your tongue man", MacIain spat out. "When you are here in Campbell Town it is best to say nothing".

They passed the Tolbooth, where MacIain had been held, a

prisoner, nineteen years ago, and from where he had made his escape, before being brought to trial. An event, which had contributed to the legend he had now become. He vividly remembered that he had not relished facing the judgement of a jury on which every man empanelled, to serve, bore the name Campbell.

With care the Chief arranged for the three of them to lodge in a small inn a mile or so out of the town. There were no other guests, so their privacy was sheltered.

"Neither of the two of you shall leave this place without me, for your own safety. It is necessary that I go to enquire as to taking the oath with Ardkinglass, you will stay here", the Chief informed them.

Angus protested vehemently. But, MacIain calmed him

There was no sign of the Sheriff and enquiries only yielded the fact that he had gone home to be with his family for Hogmany. There was no word as to when he would return. In the Chief's heart the remnants of hope, that had fluttered ragged in the gusting winds of passing time, were crumbled to dust. All he could do now was wait.

Wait they did, the passing of time interminable. Slowly it dragged on. They were boxed in by it, held tight within its pincers. Each morning MacIain made his way, alone, to the Court-house, to find out if Ardkinglass had returned, and again about the third hour after noon, but to no avail. It would seem that the Sheriff-Depute was delayed either by the weather or the celebrations, or a combination of the two.

At last on the fifth, the Sheriff was back.

He sat there in his solid oak chair. Abundant lank hair surrounded his domed forehead, with a drooping moustache and a world weary bloodhound's face, which combined to make him ageless. Yet, he wore the mantle of power with an easy grace. His reputation was that he was slow, steady and relentless in pursuing matters of law, but given to fairness. He was a lover of books and no mean poet.

He nodded, his expression neither friendly nor hostile.

"What brings you here MacIain?"

"I have come to take the oath to King William, sent by Colonel Hill of Fort William, where I went to take it. But he did not have the authority".

"Man you have had ample time. The fact of the matter is that you are out with the period allotted, in which case the law must take its due course. There is no way I can accommodate you now. In everything there is a need for punctuality and you, for reasons best known to yourself, chose to delay. Your foolishness in defying the government can only redound on your own head. I know that you are stubborn, but I never took you for a fool."

Tension strummed between them, taunt as a drumhead. Neither spoke. Each looked into the others eyes, each seeking different answers.

Chastened somewhat MacIain proffered Hill's letter.

With care, as if sifting the meaning from every word, Ardkinglass read it. After an age he looked up.

"That you did present yourself, at the Fort, I have no doubt. The Governor makes that plainly clear, however, the facts are, first, you delayed the Oath taking, second, you made little or no attempt to ascertain the correct place at which to swear, in which case I see no reason as to why I should administer the Oath".

As icy rain would the words beat on MacIain's brain, his spirits plunged and there was the ache of despair in his guts. At once the room grew cold. A hiatus of silence grew, hanging in the chill. It went on. Both men were lost in thought.

"Ardkinglass, I give you my word that every last man of Glencoe will swear if you deem it necessary. Those that do not will either be sent to fight in Flanders or be shipped for transportation".

"They tell me that at Achallader you were threatened with a mischief by the Earl of Breadalbane. Was that the case?"

Knowing that there was little love lost between Ardkinglass and Breadalbane, MacIain wondered where this tack would lead?

Indeed The Sheriff, had been instrumental in leading the opposition when Breadalbane had made a play for the Chieftainship of Clan Diarmid, being of the old school who believed in Chieftainships being in the direct bloodline. There were also other Campbell Clan politics, back in the mists of time, of which MacIain had no knowledge.

"Indeed he did"

"And you were warded in the Black Castle, whilst on your way here, and released the next day without any reason or charges having been brought against you?"

MacIain felt the first faint trembling of the thread of hope. What should he say? Was it best to remain silent? He pondered. His Clan's welfare was balanced as if on the honed edge of a dirk

Before he could say anything the Sheriff spoke.

"He who lies down with dogs gets up with fleas", he said. "In view of the fact that you did journey to Fort William, corroborated by Governor Hill, and that you have journeyed from there, beset by the worst of weather, and that you appear to have been held, in a manner, which could be deemed unlawful, I am mindful to administer the Oath, with the proviso that it be ratified by the Privy Council.

With no further ado the Oath was taken.

"I will forward certification of this, together with a copy of Colonel Hill's letter to Edinburgh, for the Council. Also, I will write to Colonel Hill instructing him to afford you and the people of Glencoe all protection, until the will of the Privy Council is made known"

Business now being finished Ardkinglass poured, from a stoneware flask, two measure of whisky.

"Drink that man, for I am thinking you have need of it".

That it was amongst the best he had ever had the old Chief freely admitted, Classic Perthshire, which had been matured for an age in an oak cask, a complex of malt, peat-reek, with a dry roundness and a depth of taste, full of flavour.

XXXIX. THE MASSACRE.

As it soared the eagle noticed, almost at the extreme extent of its vision, a movement in red. At once its eyes refocused, the fovea altering to increase the visual acuity from that of four times better than that of man to six times better. At the same time the pecten altered to give a heightened perception of shapes. Interest increased, the bird went north keeping the subject in view as it approached. Two thousand feet below it and at two miles distance it had discerned that the redness was that of man, marching soldiers, their uniform a stain of scarlet on the snow, red ants about their business, moving with a rhythmic intensity, below the immensity of the mountains of Glencoe. Man meant danger, so the eagle side- slipped left and rose effortlessly into the sky, turning in great circles, as the wind in its wings lifted it higher and higher. There was more important business to be about; up on the slopes, on open ground, between the snow-fields, it could take a mountain hare.

At the first sighting of the troops a runner was sent at all speed to alert MacIain's sons, MacIain himself being off to Dalmally. In no time atal Iain and Alasdair had made it down to the foot of the Glen, accompanied by about a score of clansmen they had gathered on the way.

On they came, with the tramp of armed men, measured and with the steady cadence of troops schooled to beat it out with regimental evenness. At their head, in command, was Robert Campbell of Glenlyon. As they came level with the men of Glencoe an order rang out. As a body, in unison, the column halted.

"So, it is yourselves, Iain and Alasdair, a good day to you both".

"And where would you be going and why", Alasdair asked of his wife's uncle?

"I have papers, here, from the Governor of the Fort, which set it all out. However, it will be quicker if I explain it to you". This he said whilst smiling in a friendly manner. "His Majesty's forces have been ordered to proceed against Glengarry, who, despite being cautioned to the contrary, has proceeded to fortify his Castle, in which case he is deemed to be a rebel. Therefore, he is to be dealt with accordingly. As Fort William, at present, has a compliment of eleven hundred soldiers, it is necessary for the Government to have the hundred and twenty troops, I have with me, billeted in Glencoe".

Iain, knowing that they could not refuse to lodge the men, asked that they be stood at ease for an hour or so, in order to allow him to send word to the chief man of each clachan to allow preparations to be put in hand to receive them.

Glenlyon, considering this to be a perfectly normal request replied, "The lads will be pleased to have a rest and, anyway, it is best that they be allotted as you think fit, for we would not want our hosts to be overburdened with too many lodgers. They are a hardy squad and straw in a byre will suffice for sleeping".

So, it was arranged.

That evening, having returned from Dalmally, MacIain held a meeting with his Chiefs to discuss the situation. They were careful to arrange it so that none of the guests was privy to what was said.

Four main decisions were arrived at. **First**, that word would be sent to Glengarry, the Chief of the MacDonells of the Clan Ranald of Knoydart and Glengarry, of what had occurred. And, that Coll MacDonald, Chief of the Keppoch MacDonalds, should also be informed. **Second**, that every man in the Glen, should be instructed to secrete their arms, in order to prevent them being requisitioned by the army. This, as intelligence had it that the Garrison, in the Fort, was short of weapons. **Third**, that any family who so wished, should have its daughters taken to Appin, for safe keeping, by the Clan Stewart. **Fourth**, that MacIain would be furnished with lists of how many soldiers had been allotted to each household, so that he could review them, and, if he thought fit, call for any relocations to prevent any household being overburdened.

"Was every Sergeant a bastard?" Trooper Sneddon asked himself.

Each morning Sergeant Barber paraded the men at Achnacon, and drilled them until they dropped, which took around two hours. Usually a session ended with a prolonged period of marking time on the spot, which was very fatiguing and resulted in several men falling out, which only served to mark them for future punishment by the big barrel-chested Sergeant, who would later allocate them further duties. He was a bully and a cynic who did not seem to believe in anything worthwhile, except, perhaps the Army, which was so fashioned as to give free rein to his ideas of discipline. There was not much that the soldiers could find in him to like. He was tall, dark-haired, surly, with a saturnine face, and his eyes were insolent, glowing with a strange light. His delight was to drive new recruits to the edge of exhaustion. When he was in a cold fury, which was not infrequent, there was nothing more terrifying. Then, the power emanating from him seemed to surpass even that of God. When he spoke his voice was sometimes laced with threat, deep and jangling to the nerves, full of verbal barbs, designed to prick and hurt. Words to him were weapons. His was the speech of a demagogue. In particular he had an obsession about the condition of muskets. Every man's weapon had to be immaculate at any time of night or day. Woe betides any person whose gun bore a speck of dirt. Every barrel had to gleam. No metallic part must bear rust, and every powder flask must be dry.

Sneddon wondered if Barber, in his dreams, had nightmares about omnipresent dust?

Every afternoon, much to the delight of the troops, they had a program of sports, which had no input from the Sergeant. Each evening MacIain and Glenlyon drew up the list of events to take place the next day. Sometimes it was a shinty game between the men of the Glen and the men of Argyll's Regiment, or an athletic competition, comprising of running, tossing the cabar, the broad leap, the high jump, wrestling and throwing the stone. Conviently Glenlyon had had a sixteen pound cannon ball brought for just such a purpose. At running no one could match Riggan Og, whether it be long distance or a hundred yards dash. One of the soldiers proved to be best at both the broad leap and the high jump. Much to almost everyone's chagrin Sergeant Barber, who was of a build to suit shot putting, proved to be outstanding at that event. His best throw being two and a half feet further than anyone else's. MacIain's son Alasdair seemed to be the best wrestler, his height of nineteen hands giving him the advantage.

Mac Iain announced that he would put up a prize, of a dirk made by MacNab, the Dalmally Smith, for the man adjudged as the best performer, at an athletic event, the next day. Expectation was heightened, for Dalmally dirks were much sought after. The judges were to be Glenlyon, one of the Lindsays and Iain Og.

With the coming of a thaw the snow had receded up the mountains, all of the white rage gathered in the River Coe, with the melt, which ran over its spate tormented rocks in a roaring rush of impetuous waters, which sobbed uncontrollably as they went down to the sea in a seething torrent of awesome power. Above them Sgor nam Fiannaidh reared, a sheer, fractured, fall of rock, with ravens wheeling round its head, the snow clinging tenaciously to every available ledge.

As the afternoon progressed it became apparent that the prize of the dirk would lie between Riggan Og, for his running and Sergeant Barber for his performance with the cabar and the shot. It would be a difficult decision to reach, but there had to be a winner. After long deliberation it was agreed that Barber was the Winner, in particular, because of his outstanding prowess as a putter of the weight. Glenlyon made the presentation.

Perhaps, it was in his makeup, but almost at once, the Winner began to make disparaging remarks about the men of Glencoe, suggesting that they might be better to take up needlework or knit woolen socks. There were those there, especially amongst the younger lads, who would have challenged him to fight, but they had MacIain's words ringing in their ears, "When any guest is in the Glen he will at all times be treated with the utmost Highland hospitality. At all times his person shall be sacrosanct, inviolate. Every hair on their heads is sacred".

"Hold your tongue, man", expostulated Glenlyon.

But Barber's dander was up and he would not.

Acnacon strode forwards, out of the crowd, the breeze stirring the two eagle's feathers in his bonnet. He walked straight up to MacIain. "Show the man", he said, picking up the shot and handing it to him.

"I have not thrown a shot for over fifteen years", said the Chief.

"For the Clan, then, show them what a real putt is".

With care Mac Iain removed his bonnet and carefully placed it on the ground, then relifting the ball he paced up to the sawdust line, which was the mark from which you had to throw. With care he took two long extended strides back, hefting the weight, in his hand, experimentally. The ball he placed comfortably at the base of his first three evenly spread fingers, with the little finger and the thumb supporting, he placed the shot against his chin, with the elbow held high. King-fisher fast he hopped forwards, the hips balanced, the rear leg extending, with the front leg stabilizing towards the line, the shoulders square to the rear, with the left arm relaxed. His right foot was pulled in, under his body to the power position. His right hip pushed through with a fast drive from the right leg, his body weight came over his left leg and his hips squared to the direction of throw, the arm struck and straightened with the elbow held tight behind the shot, which he propelled forward. The whole throw had been a gradual build up to this explosive release at the moment the weight was moving at the fastest possible speed. Up the ball soared in a graceful parabolic arc to thunk down into the turf. There was a great cheer from the crowd, for the shot had landed at a distance of four and a half feet further than Barber's best throw.

Unhurriedly the Chief retrieved his bonnet, adjusted the three eagles' feathers on it, donned it and strode off, without a word to anyone, a scad of deer hounds at heel, the dogs trailing after him, faithful, as they were vigilant.

His father, Achnacon mused, would have been proud, for he had taught Mac Iain, as a young boy, the mechanics of the putt.

Around the head of the mountain the ravens seemed to take alarm, for they became, all at once, raucous, cawing loudly, whilst flying off northwards towards the Pap of Glencoe, which thrust skyward, with its coating of snow, like a maiden's breast, as pristinely white as the belly of a Black-Backed Gull, aloof and beautiful,

"In the night the lads were cold", Jean told her husband.

"It was indeed a cold night, but sodgers should be hardened to it, when a creich is on the men sleep out in the heather, with only their plaids to wrap themselves in".

"That's as maybe, but I'm seeing that both the troopers will have an extra blanket the night".

"Suit yourself, they'll be going soft, woman", Donald responded, "Still, it was best not to argue with the wife, for she'd have the last word anyway, and the soldiers were guests".

When Alasdair told his wife, Fiona, of the quartering of the troops and that Glenlyon was in command of them she said not a word, which surprised him.

"Surely the coming of your uncle must be pleasing to you? To see the son of your Grandmother is something that you should look forward to, for now that he is in the army the chances of seeing him are few and far between".

The vehemence of her response took her husband aback.

" If I was never to see him more it would not trouble me a whit. He is evil, beyond anything you know. Have a care of him, for his presence here, in the Glen, bodes no good. Mark my words, watch him, and never trust him. In a pit of snakes, if he were there, among a hundred asps, I'd trust the serpents before him. He is devious by nature, can charm whomsoever he chooses, and, when the time comes, that suits, he can cast them down or snap them like a twig, without a single thread of compassion. To him was never given the capacity to feel pity for anyone other than himself. Hate in him is like the germs of a latent disease."

"Fiona, these are strong words. I never thought to hear them of your uncle".

"I never thought ever to use them for I never thought he would come to walk in Glencoe".

On the floor lolled a pack of large sleek deer-hounds, the colors of mist and rusted bracken, easy in their inert grace. Bran, the largest, was nearest the heat of the hearth. Without doubt he was the most intelligent, by far; when a stag was on the run, all of the others would pursue it along or up the course of a burn, but Bran would stay on the bank, never plowerting through the water, conserving his strength. He, also, unlike the others knew when to leave the trail, cut a corner, and arrive, at the place where the stag was bayed, long before any of the other dogs. He was, what those who knew dogs, called a seeing-eye hound.

When Glenlyon came, the first night, Mary had just thrown a pine log, which was perhaps damper than usual, on to the fire. There was an explosion of sparks and the dogs scattered at once. Bran yelped, burnt by a tiny, glowing ember. To reassure him MacIain bent down to fondle his ears, but was surprised to feel the dog's birse stiffen under his hand, which he then slid under its throat, and felt, there, the beginning of a silent growl.

At once came a knocking on the front door and there was Glenlyon, come to pay his respects to the Chief. He had brought a bottle of his best claret with him.

Full of good cheer he greeted MacIain and Mary profusely.

The evening progressed, the men conversing on a variety of subjects, whilst they drank the claret. Mary fed them on buttered scones with her own make of rowan-berry jam. On parting Glenlyon had a hot toddy of MacIain's French brandy, with two spoonfulls of heather honey. He left with the promise of a game of cards, the next night, with the Chief and his sons.

As they lay in bed, before sleep came, MacIain, who always valued her judgement, asked Mary what she had thought of their guest?

" For me, he is no fool, his flow of talk is easy, as is his manner, which is refined and self controlled. In short, I would say, he is personable and plausible. But, he could not hold your eyes when speaking to you, and they were full of tiny bloodshot threads, which, coupled with the web-work of veins across his nose and cheeks, tells me that he is given to drink. I suspect, Alasdair that he runs on a rich mixture of claret, brandy and uisquebach".

Each morning, whilst Barber drilled the men, Glenlyon would stroll down to his niece's house, there, to spend an hour or two before the afternoon activities. With a superhuman effort Fiona had schooled herself to receive her Uncle. It was not easy. Her husband, she knew, would not always be with her when Glenlyon came, but, as the wife of the son of the Chief, she had to do her bit for the sake of the unbending rules of Highland hospitality, which were set in stone, and she had therefor to receive whomsoever came into the Glen, as guests.

With the occurrence of the thaw the weather had improved

and it was warmer than of late, with days of fitful sunshine. To accommodate Glenlyon they had placed a chair just outside the door, with a dram of whisky, ready poured out, set to hand on a stool. The pale amber liquid caught and refracted the light, as he lifted the glass, drinking with studied deliberation and total enjoyment. He sipped the spirit slowly, feeling better and better in himself, stronger and stronger, as it went down.

It was several years since he had seen his niece. She was, indeed, truly beautiful. He was startled by the contrast between the rose-hip red of her mouth, her raven hair and her blue eyes. Her throat was the colour of the ivory seen in a print from the Book of Kells. " And, why should she not be so?" he asked himself, for her grandmother, his mother, had been considered to be one of the most beautiful women in the Highlands, a woman who had had three husbands, each a Chief. First his own father, the Campbell Chief of Glenlyon, then the Chief of Clan MacGreggor and finally Stewart of Ardsheal, the Tutor of the Stewarts of Appin.

Away to the west, above the salt water of Loch Linnhe, the mountains of Kingairloch and Ardgour climbed to the clouds, snow capped, yet rooted to the earth, filled with crumpled shadows; their faces stark and ageless. And, far off, distant, were hills, white and indistinct, phantom-like. It pleased Glenlyon's eye. He liked the purity of the raw air. His host, Alasdair Og, refilled his glass, from which he sipped slowly and lovingly. In the calm, half-asleep, he began to daydream; the dreams hanging like drifts of smoke, lingering on for a moment, before fading forever.

Best of all the troops liked the evenings, for there was entertainment for all, with several ceildhs, in every township, each night. If you felt that it would be better in another house you just left the one you were in and went to the next. The Bards were in fine fettle, all eager to prove their worth as a story teller, a reciter of poems, or best of all to prove that their own poems were better than anyone else's. All of the pipers, good and bad, were there to play, men of the Glen or anyone from the army who wanted to try their hand. There was dancing, reels and schottisches, and sword dances, and through it all ale was on tap. There was also the added bonus, for the soldiers, that they could, within the bounds of propriety, speak with the women and join them in a dance without causing too much offence with their men folk.

Sometimes there was aggravation between a family and the troops billeted in their home, though nowhere was it as bad as in the household of Achnacon, the Chief man in the clachan of Achnacon, for that was where Sergeant Barber had been billeted. There was no cogent reason for it, nothing apparent, but at the first meeting between the two, there had been instant animosity, a mutual dislike. Neither could have said what it was based upon, but both knew it was there. Along with Barber there were four troopers, whom the sergeant treated with total disdain. At every moment of the day they were at his beck and call. His delight was to inflict on them the most menial of tasks and all manner of degradation. This in turn fuelled Achnacon's dislike further.

Many a time, in conversation with Donald Clinair, Lady Glencoe's uncle, a warrior of great repute, who had served in the Spanish Army, Achnacon had heard of what Sergeants were. According to Clinair they had personalities stronger and more wilful than those of most men. They could bond a group of males together by the power of their character, yet still remain aloof and in control. They had to be admired and held in awe, even though they were hated. The men they commanded had to feel, despite everything, that they'd follow the bastard into Hell and back. They had to be firm and uncompromising. Above all else, for them, the Regiment came first, the individual second. A Sergeant made stupid orders, from Officers, work, and, stupid soldiers, below, give of their best and surpass themselves.

Each night Glenlyon would come to the Chief's house to play cards, sometimes with MacIain's sons, or alternatively he would bring his brothers – in – law, the two Lindsays. Usually the game was Ombre, with four players. Glenlyon was good, MacIain's sons allowed. He had a card-sharp's eyes, but behind them was the washed pebble opalescence of one who drinks, to whom alcohol is all, to whom the essence of the grape and the spirit of the grain was necessary, before all else.

As each evening progressed the drink flowed, Glenlyon's claret and MacIain's brandy. It was hard not to notice that Glenlyon would quaff the brandy before the red wine. Perhaps, the stronger the alcoholic content, the better the drink? He was a practised gambler, but with the drink in him and his greed fed, he would become reckless and throw caution to the winds, if he thought he could take the pot.

Knowing just how good MacIain was, as a player of the game of Ombre, Alasdair saw that on many occasions his father, without anyone noticing it, shed trump, when there was no need to, or led the second highest card, in a suit, allowing Glenlyon to take the trick, and reserving lower value cards to be played later, when the chance, of taking a trick with them, had gone. If MacIain had so chosen, he could have retained the advantage of the Bank, by virtue of his phenomenal memory, which made him such a fine card player. At all times, without conscious thought he knew every card which had been played and those which still had to fall; as well as having the ability to recall, even after years, the layout of a particular piece of land he had visited, and how many cattle it could carry. Put to it, the Chief could have, at a sitting, emptied his guest's money poke. He chose not to do so.

At the end of each evening when it was time to go Glenlyon would take his leave, going off with the uncertainty of a weaving step, having trouble negotiating himself through the doorway.

Without a word the Lady Glencoe would look at her husband, raise her eyebrows and purse her lips.

In a humorous tone MacIain would say, "Woman, but it is right to defend the stomach against the night mist; what better way than a wee dram for that?"

On the first evening on which the Lindsays came to play at MacIain's house they were pleasantly surprised at the degree of sophistication they found, for, being Sassenachs they were, to some extent, to say the least, conditioned to believe that Highlanders were primitive. Candles were lit to give the light, not fashioned from cheap tallow but made from beeswax, there was a good going peat fire, whose reek perfumed the air with its wonderful fragrance. There were no lime washed walls, each room was panelled with pine, and each window was paned with French glass, unique in the Glen, for most windows were either glazed with hornblende or simply had wooden shutters, which were closed at night to keep out the cold.

On the longest wall, in the main room, hung one of the Chief's most prized possessions, the tapestry Mary had sewn for him, as an engagement present. In the upper left hand corner was the head of a highland bull, with its great sweep of horn; in the right- hand - upper the head of a golden eagle, proud and fierce. Below, were five bunches of heather, three on two, to symbolise MacIain's descent from Iain Abrach, John of the Heather. So realistic and so true were the colours of the plant that one could believe, that, if you strode through the glory of the purple the disturbed pollen would rise to fill your nostrils with its scent. Beneath the main window was a great carved wooden box, Mac Iain's Wedding Chest, in which the Lady Mary stored her linen.

With studied care the younger brother seemed to make, surreptitiously, a mental inventory of each apartment, though the Lady Mary noted every move, Indeed, he did, for he quickly noted MacIain's silver drinking quaich, the silver punchbowl, with its delicately worked silver ladle, and, on the fingers of Lady Glencoe's remarkable hands, for which she was known, far and wide throughout the Highlands, by having a proverb attributed to her, when anyone wanted to place emphasis on the colour of white, "As white as the Hands of the Lady Glencoe". But, Lindsay was not interested in the colour of her hands or their delicacy, but in the rings on her fingers, three in number. There was her engagement ring, a plain silver hoop engraved with the MacDonald badge and the Clan slogan, her wedding ring of gold, fashioned with a pair of clasped hands and the motto, "Heart of my Heart", and the third was an "eye" ring, with an onyx which had been cut across its layers of colour to give the appearance of a human eye, which winked in the peat-fire flame.

Early in the morning the entire Company of Troops was paraded at Achnacon, after which they were marched off on a twelve mile route march, by way of Invercoe, Ballahulish, and on towards Kintallen. They halted about the six-mile mark and were addressed by Glenlyon.

After a rest they returned, by the same route, to the Glen. Dark grey, heavy, tumescent clouds, by now abounded, presaging snow. As they returned the troops marched with the demeanour of a cortege; the sound, echoing between the mountains, was of iron studded boot heels driven in, not a word was passed between the men. It seemed as if they were thirled, in some way, to a secret, the knowledge of which was hard to bear. In the Glen the soldiers appeared to evade eye contact with anyone with whom they had become acquainted. After they were dismissed most of them went back to their billets, or drew together, in groups, conversing in hushed tones, with all talk ceasing should a MacDonald appear.

Quickly, word spread that two men, who had been lodged with Achtriachtan,. had been placed under close arrest on the charge of mutiny, on Glenlyon's orders they had been marched off to Inverlochy, under close guard.

There was no specific word as to the details of their offence.

As was usual, on a Friday, MacEunrigh the Piper, held his piping class at the Grey Stone, at Achnacon. Anyone could come either to play or to listen. Some of the soldiers, particularly the Highlanders among them, would take a try at the pipes. Arthur Farquhar was perhaps the most accomplished of them. When it was his turn he struck up into "Women of the Glen", a tune often played as a portent of things to come. His piping was full of melancholy regret, the notes softly sobbing to the heights. The haunting music faded, but the heartbreak it spoke of lingered long. With little ado he turned, tucked his pipes under his arm and paced over to the grey boulder. There he stopped, and in an undertone addressed it, "Grey Stone of the Glen, yours is the right, before all others, to be here. Yet, if you kent what would happen this nicht, you would gird up your hurdies and be off out of it". There were those of the Glen who heard. At once he strode off, talking to no one, and quickly disappeared.

On Friday, the thirteenth of February,the next day, they would celebrate the festival of St.Bride. officially the first day of Spring, though in the Glen the God of Winter still held sway. Great the excitement, especially amongst the young. In each home a sheaf of oats, dressed in woman's clothes, would be laid in a creel, which the maidens would dance round and sing the song of welcome to Bride, the Godess of Spring. Then there would be feasting, if the food supply allowed, and a great coming and going between households, with friends meeting friends. She was the patroness of poets, blacksmiths, healers and above all to cattle.

"Let's have a turn at the Basset tonight, for I've just had my pay and I feel that luck is with me", said Glenlyon. His the hope to tap into the vein of gold all gamblers dream of.

So, it was agreed.

For the first time, in nights, they would use all fifty two cards, each man to be dealt a full hand of thirteen, unlike Ombre, which was played without the sevens, eights and nines of every suit.

There was a heightened tension in the room, greater than at any time they had played Ombre, for the risk, in the game, was considerable, for great losses or great gains might occur. With the run of the cards and having the nerve, if Soissante was achieved, the fifth win on the same card, without the player having taken previous payment, on it, it would yield a return of sixty seven times the original wager, the highest possible win. Advantage lay with the Talliere, the Banker, who has the sole disposal of the first and last card, which gives a much greater prospect of winning.

The cut gave Glenlyon the Bank, but adroitly MacIain had soon become Talliere. Hand after hand they went on, through the evening. With care Iain and Alasdair were able to keep their loses to a minimum, but, Glenlyon had amassed a not inconsiderable pot of twenty nine guineas, which, both sons felt, their father was biding his time to acquire.

Claret and brandy flowed, which, together with his winnings, put Glenlyon in a jovial mood.

Unexpectedly, there was a loud hammering at the door which caused the deerhounds to bark. A soldier entered. His face was blue with cold and there was snow on his boots. His eyes found Glenlyon, whom he saluted. "Urgent despatches for you Sir, brought by a rider from the Fort. You are to open and read them at the soonest opportunity".

Rising from his seat the Officer-Commanding, in extreme haste, with a muttered apology, threw his cards down and was off out of the door. The cards fell face down, all save one on which the red rhomboids seemed to throb and pulse in the flickering candlelight, like scarlet droplets of fresh blood shed on a ground of white. It was the nine of diamonds

An awful coldness settled about Alasdair's heart, the hair on his forearms came erect. The chill gripped him within and without, as only ice can do, freezing his spirit. The cold in the room clutched at him. All of his fears coalesced. A sense of impending disaster bore down on him. Unbidden the words of Angus Taish flowed into his mind. *"Tell Mac Iain that, when the white shroud of the snow is on the ground, he should have a care, of him, who had held the nine of diamonds in his hand".*

Unnoticed, the neglected pile of abandoned coins caused restless, ochreous, shadows to ebb and flow across the surface of the table.

Outside a ravenous wind rose relentlessly, steadily increasing; at first with a low, surly growl, whining in the gullies, gathering strength, until it blew with full force, insistent, fierce, filled with latent power and bearing snow.

Bran began barking furiously, and the other deer- hounds, Luath and Griane joined in. Then there came a loud hammering on the outer door. Malcom, the old servant roused himself.

"Who could that be, at this time of the morning, and on such a night of wind and snow? Maybe it was a messenger from Keppoch or Glengarry, with word for MacIain?"

With no further ado Malcom unbolted the door and opened it. Snow blew in, in a driven shower of flakes.

There were people there, indistinct in the gloom.

"Come away in out of the cold", said the old retainer.

By now the stir had awakened MacIain and his wife. With care, though still only half awake, the Chief struck sparks to light a crusie.

"What a day for the first of Spring and all the Glen waiting to celebrate the festival of St. Bride".

Talk came from the doorway, but it was garbled and overlain by the sound of the wind. Malcom stuck his head in at the bedroom doorway.

"There are two Sassenach Officers here for you. The ones you call Lindsay"

"Bring them a "morning", a glass each of the best whisky, for they will be cold, and one for myself and we will be drinking to St. Bride".

With urgency, Mac Iain started to dress, pulling on his tartan trews. He had one leg on when Lindsay entered the room. No word was spoken.

Without hesitation Lindsay presented a pair of pistols at the Chief, whom he shot in the back, as he began to turn, and then in the head. One report followed the other, sharp and loud in the confined space. Feathers of gun -smoke spurted into the air, misting the room. A seeping wound pooled blood into the bowl of his sternum. Air hissed as his punctured lungs fought for breath, and filled with fluids, a sibilant, sobbing sound. One wall was spray blasted with blood, bone fragments and pink brain matter. In an instant the chamber had become a place of death and chaos.

Lady Glencoe stood stock-still, horror struck, as her husband slumped to the floor, quite dead. Then, with unimaginable ferocity, the Lindsays were at her, tearing off her night clothes and then trying to take the silver rings from her fingers. But the could not, for her knuckles were swollen. Instantaneously, the younger Lindsay began to tear them off with his teeth. A thread of blood trickled from his sideways turned mouth, forming a small pool beneath his left cheek.

Without compunction they shot Old Malcom and his wife and then turned MacIain's wife out into the snow, stark naked.

In the darkness, all up and down the Glen the killing went on, on this the first day of Spring, on this the day of the Festival of St. Bride, whose personal text was "Blessed are the merciful, for they shall obtain mercy". Iain, the Chief's son had been forewarned by soldiers, and had managed to flee to safety, up the slopes of Meall Mor, accompanied by his brother Alasdair and his family. Their knowledge of the ground and the drifting snow aided their escape.

At Inverigan, Inverigan himself, along with eight other men, was bound and gagged. Glenlyon supervised the operation. With aclarity the prisoners were dragged outside, into the snow, to be killed in cold blood. Glenlyon shot Inverigan.

At Achnacon, four men were shot dead as they sat at the fireside. Achnacon and his brother, who had been wounded, asked Sergeant Barber if they could be allowed to die out of doors? Barber, with a sneer, said they could as it would save having to clean up any mess afterwards. They stood Achnacon against the gable end, but, adroitly, he was able to throw his plaid over the soldiers' muskets, and, in the subsequent confusion, to run off, with his brother into the darkness.

At Leacantium Archibald MacDonald, an old man of over seventy was dragged from his bed and clubbed with musket butts and left for dead. Later he was able to crawl to the safety of another house, but, being observed, the troops fired the thatch and burnt him to death. His son, Richard managed to escape.

Aided by their intimate knowledge of the terrain and, not infrequently by having had secret hints from soldiers, or, in some cases, by recieving direct assistance, many of the people were able to escape to safety, though an unknown number of the old, the very young or invalids died of hypothermia, freezing to death up on the heights. Perhaps the greatest factor contributing to the final count of only thirty eight killed was the fact that Lieutenant Colonel Hamilton, in bringing a company, from Inverlochy, by way of the high tops, over the pathway known as the Devil's Staircase, was severely delayed by the fallen and falling snow, which resulted in his subsequent failure to block the passes. He did not come down into the Glen until nine of the morning. By this time there were few MacDonalds left to slay, only an occasional invalid or a wounded man. Around noon the slaughter was over, the houses fired and the livestock rounded up to be driven off to Inverlochy, where they would later be sold, and the prize money earned would be distributed to the troops. In all they had nine hundred cattle, two hundred horse, and a motley collection of sheep and goats. Inscrutable the hills stood, For centuries they had endured the passage of time and the weather; seeing all, laconic, water washed and frost-burst. One of the Lindsays walked with a limp for in the toe of his left boot were the rings of the Lady Glencoe. His brother had in his knapsack the silver drinking quaich and its ladle.

Wrapped in oiled silk Glenlyon still had the order -

> *"You are hereby ordered to fall upon the rebels, the MacDonalds of Glencoe, and put all to the sword under seventy. You are to have special care that the old fox and his sons do not escape your hands; you are to secure all avenues that no man escape. This you are to put into execution at five of the clock, precisely; and by that time or shortly after it, I will arrive to be*

*at you with a strong party. If I do not come to you at five, you
are not to tarry for me, but to fall on. This is by the King's special
commands, for the good and safety of the country, that these
miscreants be cut off root and branch. See that this be put into
execution without fear or favour, or you may expect to be dealt
with as one not true to King or Government, not a man fit to carry
a commission in the King's service. Expecting you will not fail
in the fulfilling hereof, as you love yourself. I subscribe to this at
Ballachulish, the twelfth of February, sixteen hundred and ninety
two".*

    Robert Duncanson.

By now Glenlyon had drunk a bottle and a half of claret and also some brandy. The fog of alcohol had blurred the edges of his conscience, helping him to face his demons and life itself.

He mused, "what a wonderful thing, the Chain of Command, forged and tempered on the anvil of time, made sacrosanct, to afford Commanders glory if victory was theirs, or even better, an escape from blame if defeat occurred or things went wrong. The longer the Chain, the harder to pin the blame for mistakes. A most wonderful thing the Chain. It went from Hill to Hamilton to Drummond, to himself, and most importantly, it had emanated from the King, who might have signed it unknowingly or uncaringly, and to the Master of Stair, the Secretary of State, and, though it would never be able to be proved, to that most devious of men, the man who owned him, Breadalbane. What was important was that the chain link-of-fear, on which all despotism depends, should not be broken. Would the bowl of water be brought to the throne and the hands rinsed?"

Over, to the left, a young trooper stood, tears streaming down his face.

"Here, have a pull at this man", said Glenlyon, proffering his bottle, "Wine for solace and, perhaps, repentance".

On the previous day Lachlan had gone up on to the heights, after retrieving his hidden gun, to see if he could shoot a few ptarmigan, to be used to eke out the food supply, which was running low, as a result of he and his wife having had two soldiers billeted on them.

He knew that early in the morning the birds would move downhill to feed, above the tree line. Only a full blizzard would cause them to go lower. Now, at this time of year, the ptarmigan were all white in their winter plumage, the cocks having a black tail. When they ran on snow they were, for all-the-world, like grey stones moving, almost invisible. Their preference was to run and hide rather than to fly. However, in flight, they were wonderfully swift. If there had not been the imperative to take them against a need Lachlan would have shot them on the wing, but of the five and a half brace he only hit three birds in flight, the rest were on the ground.

At one point, where the wind had stripped the ground bare of snow, he had unexpectedly come upon a conference of mountain hares. Quickly, he had tried to unsling his gun and fire, but he never got the shot off. Round the shoulder of the hill came an eagle, flying with purpose, seeking its breakfast. At the sight of Lachlan it had side slipped left, at considerable speed, and dropped down into the immense bowl of a corrie, its rate of going increasing with the pull of gravity. In a heartbeat it was gone, lost in frosted silver and palest tourmaline, gone into an abyss of pearly light.   Now for home, off he set, the birds heavy in his game bag, but Elsepeth would be pleased, for she could vary the soldiers diet, with soup or the meat. His thoughts were on his wife and their child to be. Poignantly, he recalled the first time he had ever set eyes on her at the summer shielings, up on Rannoch. At the first sight he had taken wonder from her, so acute that it had laid a mantle of happiness on him. She had a zest for life, all of which had shone from her eyes.

As he came nearer the Glen he smelt smoke, the reek of it in his nostrils. It came, wind-borne, acrid, full of portent. Now he was at the run, down the slope.

Houses stood roofless, some on fire. He passed the body of a boy, of three summers. All about was destruction, dead hens, a loom axe-hacked, a vandalised St Bride's effigy, a smashed chair, a rope-winder broken to matchwood, a grindstone sundered in three pieces, more bodies. Some part-buried in a dung midden. His own house was a smoking ruin, the walls fallen in, the roof fired, a husk, which had succoured his family for over eighty years before it had been violated. Then he found Elsepeth. She hung, spreadeagled, pinned to the door by a bayonet. The musket, to which it was attached, abandoned by its owner. Her eyes were still as bright as the periwinkle. At the insistence of the wind the hanging wing of her hair moved gently across her face, caressing it. On the ground, beneath her tiny droplets of blood glittered, now frozen carmine, gelid, ice crystals. Her unborn child had died eight minutes before her, the bayonet having pierced right through its tiny heart.

His eyes were wells of pain. His the grief.

At the departure of the soldiers MacIain's sons came down off Meall Mor to assess the situation, striding, at times, through hip deep alabaster drifts. Before them, hares started up and ran for safety, like white rags, wind blown over the snow.

All of the Glen was blue-white and merciless. Their breaths hung in silver plumes, in the cold, whilst frozen air clawed at their lungs. Behind them, in small clouds, minute, stirred up ice-motes drifted.

With all speed they made their way to Polvaig, their father's residence, at Carnoch. As they entered the black raven wings of death seemed to rustle in the dark recesses of the house. On the floor, with one hand touching his much prized wedding chest, they found the body of the Chief. In a corner, to where she had crawled, after the soldiers had gone, they found their mother clinging to the remnants of life. Her eyes were unseeing. There was no recognition, for, she was in catatonic shock, which had been caused by the release of excessive quantities of adrenaline and endocrine into her bloodstream, resulting in an interruption in her autonomic nervous system, disabling the voluntary control of her bodily functions, deranging the senses when the terror and the horror of the slaying of her husband had usurped the dominion of her mind, leaving twilight shadows buried in the recesses of her soul.

They saw that she was near to death.

Quickly, they wrapped her in two plaids and carried her away to what they hoped was a safer place. Once they had snugged her down and left her in womens' care they returned to see to their father, accompanied by two others.

Carefully, and with all due reverence, fearful of the troops return, they bore Mac Iain off, and, when they considered it to be safe, they interred him by covering his body with rocks, so that foxes and dogs and wild animals could not get at him. And, in the feverent hope, that later they could have him taken over the water of Loch Linnhe, to be buried in the sacred soil of Eilean Munde.

From high up and faraway, from Lunna Shun, the Tarn of the Red-throated Diver, came the call of a loon, the loneliest and most hauntingly beautiful ululation to be heard in all of the world..

Night came and Mac Iain's deer hounds gave his death croon to the moon. As they bayed the spicules of sound soared skywards, slow melodic pain; there, to be splintered and sundered amidst the chutes of scree, on the Anvils of the Mists. There, to sleep silently, in sorrow, in the streams of stone, for all eternity.

Wind rose to fire the thatch and timber embers, and spewed cinder dust across the face of the land, sullying the pristine white of the snow beds with ugly, dark drifts of ash. Oxygen fed the flames, which leapt ever higher, cleansing and purifying ---------- the voracious, insatiable flames of wrath.

Lightning Source UK Ltd.
Milton Keynes UK
15 October 2010

161315UK00001B/49/P